SHADOWS

of the

PAST

RODERICK A. JONES

CONTENTS

Chapter One

It's a warm Friday night in September. Greg's getting off from work about eleven o'clock at Titus Transportation in Redwood Springs, Georgia. He parks his loaded truck and shuts off the engine with a long sigh, "I'm glad this damn work week is over." the man mumbles, relieved.

The driver opens the door and gradually steps down from the vehicle. He secures it with his key and mysteriously hears people talking behind the trailer.

Greg turns around, and sees three men yelling at a young guy in the alley.

The aggressors in suits appear to be bullying a teenager.

The driver observes them curiously, pacing to the rear of the van. He veers his eyes slightly to the right, and spots a fourth guy dressed the same as the other three.

This gray-haired bystander is leaning against a black Lincoln Continental. The man has a handgun resting on the hood. Greg observes the guy's glimpse in his direction, and he remains still in the fence's shadow. Slowly, the stranger standing at the vehicle returns his attention to the action.

Greg steps closer to the fence, staring the other members with him. They're shoving a short Caucasian teenager wearing a fluffy blue jacket.

Swiftly, one of the individuals snatches the young man by the collar. He pushes the frightened male back against the building.

Greg backs toward his rig, simultaneously pulling his cell phone out. He looks at the screen and sees no illumination at all. The truck driver tries to turn it on but gets no response. The voice in his Bluetooth earpiece had told him "Not connected", but he didn't have time to stop and check the device or his phone. Besides, the man forgot to bring his car charger today anyway.

Quickly, the driver looks around him and sees no else in the yard. So he returns his focus to the alley scene while putting his phone away.

Now, he sees the same man beating the little guy.

As the other three men move nearer, the truck driver fixes his eyes on the guy lifting the gun from the continental's hood. He glances in each direction of the street, seeing no traffic flowing.

Greg looks left and notices two women standing on a balcony. The streetlight is partially silhouetting their bodies, so he can't clearly see their faces.

One of them is standing by the door of an upstairs apartment, holding something moving in her arms.

Suddenly, the driver looks to his right and sees a young girl squatting behind a newspaper stand.

In the pale moonlight, he can see she's a Caucasian female wearing a blue- and- gray jacket.

Immediately, Greg turns his eyes back to the alley scene. He stares the man with the handgun moving closer to the others.

Mysteriously, the guy cocks the trigger and aims at the teenager's head. He fires instantly, and the victim drops to the pavement.

With ease, the truck driver backs away, staring the young man's corpse. He watches the vicious crew stand over the small guy's body.

As he reaches the front of his vehicle, the men start looking around them.

Greg turns and glances right to the newspaper stand. He sees the girl already running away from the area. One of the guys looks her way and hurries chasing after the female.

Instantly, the truck driver dashes back across the graveled yard stuffing his phone back in its case. He tries to escape by ducking around the other parked vehicles.

Greg reaches the fence on the other side of the lot. He races to the rear of a parked trailer and stops to see where the men are.

Suddenly, the man spots two of them running his way. Both are drawing handguns, and rushing towards him. Desperately, the driver dashes for the opening.

Greg's black Monte Carlo is across the street in the lot. He has a loaded handgun in the glove compartment. The driver knows the men will catch him before he gets to it, so he races for the trees behind the parking area.

Shortly, Greg reaches the wood's vast borderline. He leaps between some trees and begins creeping through the brush. The driver looks back, and sees the men crossing the lot. So he runs deeper into the forest, out of the moonlight's gleam.

Greg reaches a larger tree and conceals himself behind it. He peeks at the guys silently as they search for him in the darkness. The driver remains still as they pass through the lighted path. He watches them do this several times, wading through the weeds.

Strangely, Greg observes the two tucking their guns away. He watches them talk for a moment as they step into the trail. The driver waits catching his breath until they head out of the area.

Quickly, Greg stands and takes off his coveralls. He cuffs them under his arm and steps from behind the tree. The driver watches the men as they approach the rear of his car. He sees one of the guys bending down to see his license tag as they proceed across the lot. They also look at the plates of the other two cars.

Greg observes quietly as they move back to the huge fence of the truck yard. He stares them joining the ones who'd chased the young girl.

The group converses a moment and then turn their attention to the approaching black sedan.

When it arrives, they get in quickly.

The automobile steers his way, so he hurries back to hide. He stoops down into the brush surrounded by darkness.

Greg waits a few seconds and sees the car swerving into the lot.

Gradually, it moves along with the windows rolled down.

He watches its brief stop and remains silent to see what they're up to.

After a few minutes, the car slowly moves on. It accelerates to normal speed after pulling back onto the roadway.

Greg returns to the edge of the woods again. He looks to his left at the black sedan's brake lights as it approaches the four-way intersection.

The car halts briefly, glaring the brake lights.

Then suddenly the vehicle turns left squealing its tires. It races out of sight as a couple of stray vehicles pass on the opposite side.

The driver returns his attention to the area of the murder. He spots a police cruiser pulling into the alley. "Damn." Greg sighs worrisomely, "I'm just tryin' to make it home. - I don't need to be in this situation."

He stares the officer's vehicle gradually approaching the victim's body. It stops, and Greg steps out the woods pulling his keys from his pants pocket.

Just as the policeman gets out of the car, he creeps to his automobile a few feet away.

The driver gets there, and removes his blue ball cap. He tucks it with the coveralls, and fingers through the ring for the ignition key. Greg finds the right one and hurries unlocking the door. He opens it and tosses his garments in the back seat.

While getting inside, the driver sees another police car coming down the street on his left. The vehicle has the bar lights on heading straight towards him. Instantly, Greg becomes frustrated and tries to appear normal. He proceeds to start his car without looking at the cruiser. Just as he turns on his headlights, the policeman pulls into the parking lot in front of him.

Greg remains calm as the officer steps out of the vehicle.

The policeman walks around the rear of his cruiser and slowly approaches the driver's- side window, shining a flashlight on him.

Greg rolls down the window as the officer lowers the beam to the ground, "Can I help you, sir?" he says to the officer.

"I need to see your license and registration please." the policeman asks.

Greg shoves his hand inside his right pocket and pulls out his wallet. He opens it and removes his license, then hands it to the officer.

As the man takes it from him, Greg opens his glove compartment and reaches inside to retrieve the other requested document.

The policeman looks at them closely, and hands them back. "So you're at 1224 Ralston Avenue." the officer says, and glances to the alley where the other cruiser is.

Shortly, the officer turns back to him. "What are you doing out here this time of night?"

"I've gotta' drive to my truck." Greg answers, proceeding to return his documents to their proper places, "I forgot something."

"Oh." the officer responds, "So you're a driver for Titus?"

"Yes sir." Greg answers stuffing his wallet back inside his pocket, "I've been with ''em for three years."

"You didn't happened ta' see what went on over there, did ya'?" the policeman asks, pointing to the area of the murder.

"No sir." he replies to the officer, "Just like I said, I'm just tryin' to make it home to get a shower and a good hot meal."

"Well, alright." the policeman responds, "I'm gonna' get on over there and help figure out what happened. - You have a good night, Mr. Hardison."

"You do the same, sir." Greg says and begins rolling up his window.

The officer walks away and returns to his vehicle.

Just as he pulls away, Greg stares ahead at two more squad cars. They're joined by an ambulance entering the small alley.

"I don't know who those gangsters are." he utters with a pause, "And I don't want them to know me."

While watching, he feels for his seat belt and straps it on. Greg shifts the car in gear with a long sigh of relief and pulls across the street heading back to his truck. He knows he has to get something out of it to validate his excuse to the policeman. So Greg drives into the truck yard and gets his large portable cooler out of the rig.

After doing so, he heads back out of the area and stops. Greg gets out and secures the yard's main gate with its master lock. He glances at the alley one more time while getting back in the car, "I hope this situation doesn't come back to haunt me." Greg mumbles to himself while shutting the car door.

Gradually, the driver shifts the vehicle to drive. He takes a final glimpse around him, stormed by troubling thoughts.

Suddenly, Greg picks up his pace and steers right onto the roadway. He accelerates quickly heading on to the intersection.

Chapter Two

Greg is on his way down Eighth Street heading to Ralston Avenue. He's almost three blocks away, reducing his speed. The driver moves on, repeatedly checking his rear. There's no traffic behind him, so he drives the speed limit.

Greg stares ahead and spots a police car on the right. It's sitting at a gas station with the parking lights on. He observes the cruiser calmly, approaching its tail. There's a street lamp above the vehicle silhouetting inside, so the driver can't identify how many bodies are inside it.

Within seconds, Greg's close enough to see two officers in it. He passes by the vehicle and takes a glimpse in his rear view mirror.

Strangely, the driver sees them pull out behind him. He maintains his safe speed as they approach from the rear.

Greg waits to see if they'll pull him over. He observes the white cruiser trailing a car length away.

Shortly, the driver signals left to turn on Ralston Avenue. He looks in the mirror quickly and sees the cruiser turning away. So Greg moves on brushing his forehead with a palm. He breathes a sigh of relief and drops the hand upon his lap.

Just as the driver prepares to turn, he checks his rear again spotting another pair of headlights. They're closing in on him fast, so the driver accelerates and keeps going ahead. He doesn't want to lead any strangers to his home after what's happened tonight. So the trucker turns off his turn signal.

Greg observes the vehicle approaching, as it quickly tailgates him closely.

The driver watches the car behind its bright headlights, unable to identify who it is.

He continues on and passes under a street light.

The bright lamp exposes the long dark car. The strange black sedan is about a yard away from his bumper now. The driver's not sure if it's the ones that'd chased him at the truck yard.

So Greg reaches inside his glove compartment and pulls out his revolver. The driver closes the door, and lays the weapon upon the seat. Cautiously, he resumes his surveillance and moves on.

Within minutes, Greg passes Langston Branch Road. He still sees the mysterious vehicle tailing his bumper. He reaches the green traffic light at Harlan Parkway and immediately turns right flooring the gas pedal.

The driver observes the vehicle behind him doing the same. He's pulling away from it, moving farther by the second. Greg excels to almost seventy miles per hour. He spots an apartment complex up ahead on the left.

In haste, the driver slams on the brakes and steers into it. He hurries through the area, racing through the aisle.

Immediately, Greg goes around the bend and skids to a stop. He shuts off his headlights and backs into a parking space between the other cars.

Quickly, the driver shifts to park and ducks down to the right. He peeks over the dashboard, keeping his body out of sight.

A few seconds later, the long dark car comes around. It passes by him swiftly, surging on through the lot.

The driver waits a couple of minutes, hoping they're not on foot searching for him.

Carefully, Greg rises and shifts the car to drive. He pulls out slowly and faces the main entrance. The driver creeps on, and spots the sedan at the rear of the parking area.

Instantly, he accelerates back to the street. The man steers to the right and turns his headlights on. He floors the gas pedal in haste and races back up the roadway.

Chapter Three

Nearly fifteen minutes later, Greg arrives home. He finds his seven- year-old son's little bicycle lying in the driveway. He pulls in slowly and stops the car. The driver gets out glancing around worrisomely. He places the bike upright near the garage door.

Greg returns to the vehicle and gets in quickly. He moves up to the garage door, and turns off the engine after shifting to park. The guy retrieves his firearm from the seat.

Afterwards, he gets out in a hurry.

While locking his door, Greg hears a vehicle coming up the street. He gradually tucks the handgun in the back under his belt. The driver stares the car approaching, stepping past *his* vehicle to the lawn.

When the long automobile reaches the home, it decelerates to a stop. He stands gazing at the black Lincoln Town Car as it sits before his house. "That's enough of this mess for the night." he whispers to himself angrily, staring the vehicle with a look of rage in his eyes.

Mysteriously, Greg sees the driver window roll down.

"Hey!" He hears a man's voice call, "Come over here for a minute. My boss wants to talk to ya'!"

"You're at my house!" Greg responds strongly, "If you wanna' talk, you come to me!"

As the driver door opens, Greg hands his waist staring inside the car. He realizes the chauffer is one the guys who'd chased him earlier.

How they found out where he lives, Greg didn't know. He observes the driver closely opening the rear door on his side.

Gradually, a gray-haired man steps out wearing a dark-colored suit.

Greg watches him, instantly remembering him as the shooter in the previous alley incident.

The man paces upon his grass and begins coming toward him.

"That's far enough!" Greg voices to him bluntly, "What in the hell do you want!"

The tall man halts and glances at Greg's vehicle with an evil grin upon his face, "You work for Titus Transportation, - don't you?" he says.

"Yeah." Greg answers, "What about it?"

"Did you see anything happen around there tonight," the guy inquires, "about an hour ago?"

"No." Greg replies, "What in the hell you ask me that for?"

"I just want to know if you recognize us." the man responds with a slow glance over the shoulder to his chauffeur.

The stranger turns back with that same look again, "I'm always able to touch base with you, brothers." he says folding his arms, "So what's the price to keep your mouth shut? - It'll be a shame if you refuse my offer."

His remaining three crew members step out of the car to observe, two of them slowly reaching inside their blazers. The man lowers his arms, "And ya' don't remember anything, huh?" he asks, "If I were you, I'll do like your other black homeboys and take the payoff."

Swiftly, Greg draws his handgun and aims at the man's head. As the others pull out their weapons, he cocks it quickly, "Tell 'em to put away the guns or I'll blow your damn head off!" Greg warns the gray-haired man.

The stranger immediately orders them to holster their weapons.

The truck driver waits for the crew to secure their firearms, glancing at them over the boss' shoulder.

After doing so, Greg hears the door of his home open behind him, "You want me to call the police, honey?" his wife asks him nervously.

"No baby." he answers her, "Just go back inside and close the door. - I'll take care of this."

Greg keeps his eyes focused on the guy before him. He hears his door close and continues staring ahead, "I've never seen you before." he says to the tall man, "So get the hell off my property."

The gray-haired man smirks, "My police friend ran your tag number." he responds, "That's how I found out where you live. - I apologize for the trouble. We thought you were someone else we'd searched for earlier."

"Well, now that you've found your answer, stay away from here." Greg orders the stranger, "And don't ever come back."

The man before him smiles and turns away heading back to the sedan. He reaches the car, and looks at Greg again before getting inside. The remaining of the group does the same after the chauffeur closes their boss's door.

In haste, the black sedan accelerates and races away.

Gently, Greg returns the gun's hammer to its resting position. He lowers the weapon to his side and heads on to the porch. The driver gets there, and his wife opens the door. "Are you alright?" Janna asks him nervously.

"I'm fine, baby." He replies meeting her.

"Who were those men, honey?" she asks handing his waist.

"People we don't want to know." Greg tells her, entering the house.

"I was gonna' call the police if they hadn't have left soon." Janna says with a pause as Greg shuts the door.

Softly, the driver wraps his arm around her waist. He guides her along beside him through the living room, "I hope we didn't wake up Landon." he says to her.

"You didn't." she assures him.

"Good." Greg responds.

"Why were those men trying to start trouble with you?" his wife inquires curiously.

Greg unhands her and walks to the refrigerator. Gradually, he lays the revolver upon the counter by the sink, "They're bad men, honey." the driver says retrieving his cell phone.

The man attaches the mobile and Bluetooth devices to wall chargers nearby. Slowly, he turns back to his wife. The driver gazes into her eyes, "Here's what happened." he utters in a long sigh.

Suddenly, their attention is drawn to breaking news on the television. The anchor on the set is talking about the alley murder. Greg returns to the living room with Janna following behind him.

They enter the area and stare the video footage. When the lady mentions the victim's name, both of them bow their heads.

Lightly, Janna brushes her hand across her forehead, "Cole has never bothered anybody." she mentions pacing away, "Why would somebody wanna' kill him?"

"I know Cole had a drug problem." Greg mentions sadly, "But he's never started any trouble out there."

"He got involved with the wrong people." Janna responds facing him, "Miss Nora just got out of the hospital. - She doesn't need to hear about that."

Greg sighs and walks away with his hands upon his waist, "Some young girl was with him. - I hope she got away."

"Did she have brown hair with a Clayton High School jacket on?" Janna asks.

"Yeah," Greg utters facing her, "-how did you know?"

"She's his new girlfriend." his wife replies, "Her name is Kera Mitcham. - Miss Nora told me about her on the phone yesterday."

Suddenly, Greg recalls what happened in the alley, "That low-down bastard!" he groans in a whisper, "That son -of -a -bitch shot Cole!"

"Are you talkin' about the man who was in the yard?" Janna asks.

"Yeah, baby." Greg answers pacing away, "We may have a problem. - I don't think those guys are giving up that easily. - I've gotta' do somethin' about this. - God knows I don't want anything to happen to you and Landon. - I gave my word to you three years ago that I'll be home to you every night, unlike before. - I really don't wanna' change that."

Janna approaches him from behind and wraps her arms around his waist. "Honey?" she pauses, "Both of us understand how you hate to talk about this subject. - But you have to forgive yourself for the deaths of Rhonda and Karen. — Especially, Detective Madison. — I miss her too, and I know she was like a little sister to you. — But there's no way you could've saved them."

Greg turns around and faces his wife, "Baby, I saw that savage shoot my co-worker in the head." he explains, hugging her, "The murderer had already shot Karen in the back as she tried to get away. - If I'd have gotten there sooner, Rhonda *and* Karen would still be alive right now. — I know I shot the bastard honey. — And he still got away. — To this day, it's still a cold case. — They still don't know who was behind the black mask."

Janna caresses his waist firmly, "Greg? — You can't keep beating yourself up over that. — You quit the department because it had you stressed out. — Honey, you can't keep living with that guilt inside you."

Greg raises his hands and rests them upon her shoulders, "Karen was trying to tell me something that day at the station. - I have to figure out why she stopped talking, and suddenly had to leave. - Karen saw somebody in there that scared the hell out of her. - And to this day, I still can't figure out who it was. — There were two people in there at the time who weren't cops, Karen and a long-bearded man with Commissioner Baker. - She sped away in her car just as Rhonda got back to the station. — Detective Madison turned on her bar lights and raced after her. — If I'd have just gotten there sooner, things would've happened differently."

Just then, their attention is drawn to the news woman again. She's identifying a mob boss with an upcoming murder trial. Greg shifts Janna aside gently, and both of them stare the picture.

"Wait a minute." he mumbles, slowly pointing his finger at the screen, "That was the son-of-a-bitch standing outside just a few minutes ago."

The two of them pause shortly, gazing eye to eye.

"I got a good look at him too." Janna says, "The porch light was shining on his face. I believe you're right."

Greg steps away in thought, folding his arms. His wife moves in front of him, lightly palming his chest.

"Sweetheart?" she hesitates briefly with a sigh, "If you wanna' go back to the police department, it's okay with me."

Greg gives her a puzzling look, "You hated the long hours." he mentions, "Remember our quarrels about not having time together?"

"I know." Janna admits, "And I know *you*, honey. - You'll go after them. - If you wanna' protect us, let's do it the right way."

Greg nods with a small grin, "I'll talk to Captain Harris in the morning."

"Wait a minute." his wife lifts her index finger, "I looked at your calendar. Don't you have to work tomorrow?"

"I'll take a vacation day." he replies, "We can't take the risk of that savage coming back. - Don't worry. Let's get some sleep. - I'm gonna' take a shower, and I'll be right behind you."

"Alright." she responds stepping away and heads down the hallway.

Greg grabs his revolver from the counter and follows her into the bedroom. He places the gun on the top shelf in the closet.

While unbuttoning his shirt, he moves on to the master bathroom. The driver goes inside and gently closes the door. He stands a moment with his hand wrapped around the doorknob. Slowly, Greg bows with a long sigh. He shakes his head a couple of times, and looks up solemnly, "God?" he whispers with a short pause, "For some reason, I can feel that man's not giving up without a fight. – I'm gonna' do everything I can to stop him. – Please forgive me."

Chapter Four

About nine o'clock Saturday morning, Greg steps out the front door preparing to meet with Captain Harris. After securing the house, he straightens his navy- blue blazer and moves on to the car. The trucker feels under his arm, assuring his gun is in the holster. He pats his jacket pocket holding several loose rounds, with the remaining of a new box emptied in the other.

Greg reaches the driver side of his vehicle and unlocks the door. He gets inside, and sticks the key in the ignition.

Mysteriously, the trucker glances right and sees a black Lincoln Sedan. It's parked at the upper end of the street almost fifty feet away. He observes it while removing his phone charger from his left coat pocket. Greg stares a moment and remembers the one from last night.

In haste, the trucker stuffs the cord back inside his pocket. He starts the engine, and backs out of the driveway. Greg turns right and heads toward the car.

Quickly, the trucker approaches the strange vehicle. He brakes rapidly and shifts the car into park.

In haste, Greg gets out just as the sedan driver rolls down the window. He looks at the Caucasian man with the bushy, brown goatee. "What in the hell are you watchin' around here?" he asks him bluntly.

The guy glances at his partner next to him with a smile and turns back with an evil look upon his face, "It's none of your business." the stranger says, "At least for now."

The man smirks and then giggles with his partner.

Swiftly, Greg reaches in the vehicle and yanks the guy by the collar. He starts pulling him out through the driver's window. The man's partner rushes out of the sedan. Simultaneously, Greg draws his handgun and wraps his left forearm around the driver's throat.

As the passenger reaches inside his black blazer, Greg cocks the revolver and aims at his head.

The man hesitates and slowly moves his hand away from the coat. The passenger stares him angrily while raising his opened hands in front, "You have no idea who you're dealing with." the guy tells him, "You can get into a lot of trouble."

"Not before you do." Greg responds glancing over the man's shoulder at his neighbor, then locks eyes with the passenger again, "I'll take my chances."

"You need some help, Greg?" the elderly male resident asks.

"Yeah Mr. Grant." the truck driver replies, "Can you call the police for me?"

"I'm on my way." the old man says and rushes back in the house.

"You'll pay for this." the passenger blurts boldly, "I'll personally see that you do."

Greg stares eye to eye with the man, "Take your best shot. - But don't bother my family. - If you harm them, I'll kill you."

Chapter Five

Almost ten minutes later, Greg hears sirens approaching at both ends of the street. He has both of the men guarded with their hands resting upon the sides of their car. The truck driver glances left. He sees a police car swerving into the street then racing towards him.

Within five seconds, the guy spots another one coming in from the right.

The parked sedan's passenger looks at both squad cars, and turns back locking eyes with Greg, "You better enjoy this." he says as Mr. Grant steps back outside his door, "As I said, you'll pay for this."

Greg keeps the revolver aimed at them, "We'll see about that." he responds to the threat, "There's no fear here, man. – Bring it on. – You *and* that bastard boss you work for."

Hastily, the police vehicles halt. The officers get out and rush to the scene drawing their weapons.

When the first one approaches Greg, he stops, "What's going on man?" the policeman asks.

Greg looks at the officer, dropping his aim, "I don't think these two have permits for their handguns."

The patrolman pats him on the shoulder, "We'll take care of this." he assures.

Quickly, the policemen disarm the sedan occupants and shove them against the car. They handcuff the guys and place them under arrest.

Greg observes quietly until they're moved away to the squad cars. He returns his revolver to its holster and observes two more police cruisers coming down the street.

The truck driver stares the unmarked, maroon car with a flashing blue light on top.

While staring, he gets distracted by other neighbors coming outside.

Suddenly, Greg sees his wife approaching holding their seven- year-old son by the hand. He gives her a wave and returns his eyes to the maroon Mercury Marquis.

When Janna meets him, Greg wraps his arm around her.

"What happened?" she inquires worrisomely.

"I had a little problem with some guys out here." he explains, "I've taken care of it."

"What did they do to you?" she wonders nervously, laying her free hand against his chest.

"I've handled it, baby." he assures her, "Don't worry. - They started trouble with me, and I took care of it. - Okay?"

Janna nods and gives him a smile.

Greg returns his focus to the maroon car and notices Captain Harris coming to meet him.

The tall, slender Caucasian man in a dark suit approaches with a smile, "You can't get rid of it." he says shaking his head with a grin, "After three years, that detective is still in you."

Greg moves Janna into his left arm and shakes Captain Harris's hand, "I was coming to see you this morning, sir." he informs him.

"Good." the police superior responds with a short glimpse aside, "It appears you've neutralized this situation. And I told you about calling me sir. - It's Richard. We're friends. Remember? - You used to call me chief." The captain extends his hand and greets Janna and Landon.

"Chief?" Greg utters to him, "This situation is a lot more potent than it looks."

"What do you mean?" Richard asks, slowly folding his arms.

Suddenly, Greg's cell phone rings. He answers it and hears his driver manager's voice from Titus Transportation, "I'm sorry I haven't called you, Reese." he says, "I'm in a police situation right now. Some guys are stalking my home."

"Hey man, your family comes first." the manager responds, "They're alright, aren't they?"

"Yeah." Greg answers as Captain Harris waits patiently. "I need to take a vacation day."

"Sure man." Reese agrees, "I'll take care of it. - I'll put somebody on your runs until you get back with me. Just keep me informed."

"Thanks." Greg says, "I really appreciate it.

After exchanging good-byes, he ends the call and stuffs the phone inside his pocket.

"Sorry, chief." he apologizes.

"It's okay." Richard says, "I'm interested in what you have to tell me."

Janna pats Greg on the shoulder, "I'll take Landon back to the house so you two can talk." she suggests.

"Thanks baby." he responds giving her a light kiss upon the lips.

As she walks away, Greg returns his attention to Captain Harris, "The mobster in the news yesterday paid me a visit." he states.

"Moran!" Richard replies astounded, "Where?"

"He came on my lawn last night." Greg explains, "The man wanted to make sure I didn't see him kill Cole, Miss. Nora's son? - Moran shot him in the alley last night. I had just parked my truck when it happened."

Captain Harris hands his waist and steps away in anger, "That bastard!" he blurts out, and turns back to Greg, "A witness spotted Cole being chased from a murder scene on Grand Avenue last night. He was with some girl."

"Was she wearing a Clayton High School jacket?" Greg asks, "If so, her name is Kera Mitcham. She's was his girlfriend."

"That's her." Richard agrees, "Bill Dixon was shot and killed there Thursday night. - He was the fifth homicide in three days before Cole. The five who died before him were scheduled to testify in Moran's grand jury trial Monday. - Miss. Nora's son was just a witness to Dixon's murder. Kera walked out of the store *after* it happened. – Three bystanders confirmed that. So his girlfriend didn't see anything. – But Moran probably thinks she did because they were together."

Slightly, Greg shakes his head a couple of times, "That's sad, man."

"I know." the captain agrees, "Eyes of the innocent can put him away. And he knows that. - We have to find the girl before the same happens to her."

"You're right." Greg responds, "Moran was a little unsure about me being in the truck yard. I pretended I knew nothing about it."

"You think he saw you?" the captain inquires.

"I don't think so." Greg replies folding his arms.

"Don't bet on it." Richard advises him, "How did he find you? - Did he follow you home?"

"Yeah." Greg answers, "He said his police friend checked my tag number. There were three cars in the parking lot. - I guess they checked mine first."

Captain Harris paces away again, "I've been after that bastard for almost three years." he mentions, "For some reason, it's hard to make evidence stick to him. He has a team of lawyers from Miami defending him - six, to be exact."

Greg shakes his head again, "I don't believe he'll get away that easily this time." he says as Richard faces him again, "Not if I can help it. I'm in this deep already. - I'm a witness, remember?"

"We need to put him *and* his crew behind bars." the captain voices bluntly, "If I had your help, I know we'll find enough evidence to convict that savage. - I just wish there was some way I can persuade you to come back and work for me."

Greg looks him in the eyes, "You already have." he assures him, "Let's get on it."

Richard grins again with a light nod of the head, "I'm placing two unmarked squad cars here at your house." he explains, "One will stakeout and watch your home. The other will follow your wife everywhere she goes until we take care of this matter. - Also, let's keep Landon out of school so he can stay close to his mother."

"I planned on it." Greg concurs.

"Good." the captain utters, "This guy we're up against is desperate. He's facing a death sentence, and knows it. He'll do anything to get out of it. Meet me at the station, and we'll get started."

"I'll be there." Greg replies, "Give me twenty minutes. I have to tell Janna what's going on."

"You got it." Richard agrees, and they both step away.

Chapter Six

Greg arrives at the police precinct just after ten -thirty a.m. He's greeted by his former co-workers, and gets a warm "welcome -back" from them.

While briefly reminiscing, he spots Captain Harris stepping out of his office behind them. They make eye contact, and Richard gestures for him to follow with an index finger.

The driver asks them to excuse him, and follows the captain.

He proceeds inside the room with his former boss, and stands before him.

"Close the door." the captain says, sitting down at his desk.

Greg shuts it, and sits in the chair facing him.

"I never retired your badge." Richard responds reaching inside a drawer, "Human Resources still have you in our system - at my request, of course."

Greg gives him a puzzling look, "So my two-week resignation notice never got to payroll?"

"No." Richard says with a smile, pulling a badge out. He lays it on the desktop in front of him.

Greg nods with a grin, "So I'm still a detective."

"If you want to be." the captain replies, "I was hoping I could get you back someday. – I knew it was hard for you to accept what happened that tragic night, just over three years ago. – Sometimes I'd check on you as a friend, but I didn't want to get in your way. – I knew you needed time to grieve. So I accepted your choice to leave. – I didn't want see you go. That's why I didn't process the termination."

The driver looks eye to eye with him, "I appreciate that sir." he responds taking the badge from the desk, "And thanks for the phone calls. – Now, we've got work to do."

Richard reaches his hand across the desk to him, "Then it's official." he smiles, "Nice to have you back, Detective Hardison."

Greg shakes his hand, "Thank you, sir."

"You're more than welcomed." Mr. Harris states and releases his grip.

"How are *you* doing, sir?" the detective inquires, "When I'd ask how things were going around here, you'd hesitate – and say everything's fine. – But I could tell by listening to your voice, that wasn't entirely true."

"And stop calling me sir!" the captain reiterates in a friendly manner.

Greg giggles, "Okay, Richard."

"Twenty-sixteen has been tough on me around here." Mr. Harris admits, "I wish *you* were my lieutenant. The one I've got now is a snitch for internal affairs. - He's been a major nightmare to our men and women out there, secretly backstabbing them."

"Gaines?" Greg asks sliding back in the chair, "That definitely doesn't sound like him."

"We've got another one." the captain informs him, "Gaines was demoted a year ago with an assault charge. He floored the new lieutenant. It was a big political mess."

"Why did he hit him?" Greg inquires.

Richard leans forward and rests his elbows upon the desk. "The new lieutenant's name is Alvin Thompson." he begins explaining, "The man snatched Gaines by the collar for arresting one of Moran's men for sexual harassment. The incident took place down on Fourth and Grand Avenue. - Gaines decked him, and internal affairs busted him for giving Thompson a black eye."

"Where did this guy come from?" Greg wonders, "He wasn't here three years ago."

"The commissioner hired him, and promoted him." the captain tells him, "He started as a detective about two months after you left. I had no say-so in the matter. - I had to accept it and move on."

"We've got internal affairs running this department now?" Greg asks.

"It certainly appears that way." Richard replies leaning back slowly in his chair, "It seems like the idiots are trying to give Thompson *my* job."

Greg sighs with short bow of the head. He looks back up to the captain, "We won't let that happen. You can count on it. - I don't care what we have to do to stop it."

Suddenly, their attention is drawn to yelling outside the door. They hear a man angrily questioning one of the officers about his daughter's whereabouts. Greg and Richard gaze at each other curiously, and both get up at the same time.

They rush out the door, and lock their eyes on the desk sergeant at the entrance.

The commotion's drawing an audience of officers nearby.

A bearded middle-aged guy is arguing with Sergeant Maddox, frequently interrupted by a female companion.

From listening to her comments, she appears to be the mother of the missing teenage girl named Kera Mitcham.

"We're doing all that we can, Mr. Mitcham." Officer Maddox assures him, "Our department will let you know as soon as we find her."

Fiercely, the man points his finger at the sergeant. He continues yelling, condemning the investigation's progress.

Greg approaches him politely, "Mr. Mitcham?" he voices, holding out his hand.

The guy shakes it with a strange look upon his face, "Who are you?" he asks.

"I'm Detective Hardison." Greg replies releasing his hand, "You two must be Kera's parents, right?"

"Yes." the lady answers tearfully, "Have you heard anything?"

"Not yet," he says, "-but we'll find her. Why don't you and Mr. Mitcham come to the captain's office, and we'll discuss this matter."

The parents agree and follow him.

When they get inside, the captain closes the door gently.

Again, Greg reassures them their daughter will be found. He gets a brief description from them of Kera's hangouts and friends she visit. But Greg never gives them any sign of his true feelings of her whereabouts. He went on with his positive comments to regain their composure and trust, joined by Captain Harris.

Once they're convinced, Mr. and Mrs. Mitcham kindly shake their hands. The officers exchange good-byes with the parents and remain standing as both of them leave the room.

With a long sigh, Greg sits back down in the chair, "We have to find her, chief. I just hope she's alive."

Richard seats himself and rests his forearms upon the desk, "I don't know where to start looking for her. We have no leads right now."

Greg holds up an index finger with a thought. "We *do* have a way to find out if Moran's got her." he mentions, "If he spared her life, we have two bargaining chips."

Captain Harris nods with a smile, "The two guys we busted this morning?" he figures.

"You got it." Greg utters.

Richard opens his center desk drawer and reaches inside with a short grin, "I've got one more thing for you."

The captain pulls out a pair of silver handcuffs and slides them across the desktop to him. "I'm glad to be giving those back to you." Richard says, "You still have the key, right?"

"Yes, sir." the detective answers.

After stuffing the item inside his blazer pocket, Greg gets up. He paces to the large office window. "I've gotta' get something off my chest, sir." he exhales in a breath and then speaks on, "Karen was afraid of someone in this department. So she didn't talk and died because of it. I wish I could've saved Rhonda *and* her. - Their killer is still out there somewhere." The man faces Richard, "There was a stray black sedan at the murder scene driven by the killer. I had it impounded for the lab. They didn't find any fingerprints, DNA, or any other evidence in the car to identify the suspect - not even in the woods. - I know I shot him. They should've found something. That still bothers me to this day."

"I know." Richard replies bowing his head in sadness, "I wish I could've helped you that night. I really do. I hired Rhonda and you the same day nine years ago. I know she was like a little sister to you." he adds and looks at him, "I got both of you promoted to detectives in a couple of years. You earned it. I did the same with Kim, Rhonda's friend. All three of you are military veterans with criminal justice degrees. Upper management didn't have any problem with it. You three are like family members to me, and I love ya' man." The captain holds out a palm before him, "Sorry for interrupting. – I just wanted to mention that. – Now, go ahead. I wanna' hear the rest."

"When I met with Karen Flanningan here that night, -" Greg hesitates, "I don't know what scared her so much. - She got up and ran out of the building. I went after her, and she almost hit me with the car trying to get away." he sighs, "I only remember seeing cops here - and that guy with the commissioner wearing a coat."

Mr. Harris stands and joins him at the window.

The captain folds his arms staring him, "While you were talking to her, a long-bearded man came in *with* the commissioner that night. - It was May, and the guy's wearing a trench coat. He had hair down to his shoulders. The guy had shades on, wearing baggy clothes. I thought he was homeless." Richard mentions, "I know I've seen him somewhere. His face is so familiar. I just can't place it."

Greg takes a few seconds thinking about what the captain said. He holds up an index finger and faces him, "Wait a minute." the detective mumbles, "That guy was just standing by the hallway looking at us strangely, - especially when Commissioner Baker stepped away. "

"Exactly." the captain answers with a nod, "Waiting for the commissioner to check the vacant office."

"Chief?" Greg says folding his arms, "Did Commissioner Baker let you know he was coming that night?"

"Yes, he did." Richard responds staring him, "He wanted to use a vacant office, but didn't say why."

"Maybe he wanted to help the guy." Greg adds.

Richard points to him and starts walking back to his desk, "I should've known." he utters thinking, "I'll be damned. - If you shave his hair away, and put him in a suit, -" the captain points to the door, "He'd be that same bastard down the hallway."

Greg heads back to his seat, "You know who he is?"

Richard faces him, "His last name is Thompson." he explains, "Alvin Thompson. He may have lost a few pounds, but I believe that's the same guy."

"Let's check it out." Greg decides, "Let's see what Tara can dig up on him. - She was always the best at that."

"Good idea." Richard agrees, "None of us ever knew anything about the bastard - his past, or where he comes from. They never told us anything. The lieutenant tells us about his ravishing life in Boston. If his parents are wealthy, why in hell is he here in this police department."

"We'll find out." Greg assures him, and they leave the office.

After emerging to the open area, they look ahead towards the entrance.

Captain Harris stops and stares a bald- headed man rushing to the double- glass doors.

Richard glances at Greg, and points at the guy leaving, "That's Thompson," he tells him.

The captain goes after the lieutenant with Greg following closely behind him.

Suddenly, one of the female detectives grabs Richard's upper arm.

The captain stops and faces her. "What's going on, Tara?" he asks.

"I came out of the restroom, and heard Thompson talking to someone on the telephone." she informs him, "Whoever it was told the lieutenant that a woman mentioned seeing a murder in an alley last night. The person supposedly knows the lady, and said the tenant confessed being on her balcony when she saw it. Thompson got her address at Brookshire Apartments. I heard him repeat it."

Greg pats Richard on the shoulder, "I know where he's going chief." he tells him, "I saw two females out there last night. She's one of them."

The captain points to the entrance, "Let's try to get there before Thompson does." he suggests, "For some reason, I don't think he'll bring her back here."

The police chief races for the door with Greg following closely behind him. They dash out the front doors and scurry down the steps.

After reaching Richard's car, Greg stares him digging for his keys, "You got "em?" he asks.

"Yeah." Captain Harris answers snatching them out.

In haste, Richard unlocks the driver door. He hurries inside his Marquis and opens the passenger side for Greg.

After the detective gets in, the captain starts the car in haste. He slams it in reverse, and backs out to the street. Instantly, Richard shifts to drive and fishtails racing away.

Chapter Seven

A few minutes later, Richard and Greg arrive at Brookshire Apartments. The captain pulls in hastily and slams on the brakes by the stairwell. He shifts the car in park and they emerge from it quickly.

After slamming the door, Greg heads for the steps. He follows Richard closely, no more than a few steps behind. "She's in the last one on the right." he says, "The closest to the murder scene."

They reach the balcony and proceed to the lady's apartment door.

Greg sees Richard glancing around at the parking area down below. "What's wrong, sir?" he asks him.

"I don't see Thompson's car." Captain Harris says.

"He's probably got her and gone." Greg responds.

Suddenly, an elderly Filipino woman runs out of the apartment door crying. "You've got to find my daughter!" she screams snatching Greg by the arm, "A man grabbed her by the hair and took her away!"

"Which way did he go, ma'am?" Richard inquires.

The lady points down the street. "The man dragged her to his car and pushed her inside!" She exclaims, "I couldn't help her!"

"We'll find her." Greg assures her, "Can you describe the man?"

The lady sniffs a couple of times, wiping her eyes. "He was a white man with a bald head." she hesitates, "He put her in a silver car."

"Was he in a dark suit, ma'am?" the captain inquires, "Standing about six feet, about my height?"

"Yes." the woman answers.

"I knew it!" Captain Harris groans rushing to the stairs, "That low-down bastard!"

"Treating her like that?" Greg pauses, following him, "He has other plans for her, chief."

"I've got a strange feeling about this, man." Richard voices angrily as they rush back to his car, "I believe he's taking her to Moran! If we don't get to her, she's dead!"

The two reach the vehicle and hurry inside.

After slamming the door, Richard starts the engine. He shoves it in reverse and backs out of the parking spot. The captain shifts to drive and stomps the gas pedal, squealing the tires.

Rapidly, he steers left out of the parking lot heading down Maple Street.

"Do you think we should call for backup?" Greg suggests, "We could be heading into a trap."

"I know." Richard responds catching his breath, "Let's see if we can find the vehicle first. And I hope we won't be too late."

"We can nail Thompson for this." Greg mentions.

"I'll be glad to bust the bastard!" Captain Harris lashes out, and they glance at each other, "I'm tired of Thompson and Internal Affairs treating me like I'm some damn piece of garbage."

"Have Internal Affairs been on you that bad?" Greg wonders sitting back in his seat.

Richard looks at him and turns back to the roadway. "Those savages have been a nightmare." he groans, tightening his grip around the steering wheel.

"That's pitiful." Greg utters to him, "You've been a good boss to all of us, man."

"That means nothing to them." the captain voices angrily.

Suddenly, Richard grows silent.

Greg glances at him and slightly bows his head in sadness for him. "Things will get better, chief." he tells him calmly.

"They already have." Captain Harris responds pointing ahead, "There he is."

"Where?" Greg inquires looking ahead.

"He's in the silver Mazda 626 in front of us." Richard answers speeding towards the car.

"How did he get that dent?" Greg asks as the Mazda increases speed.

"It looks like somebody hit it with a baseball bat." Captain Harris says, "He collected the insurance money and left the damage there. The idiot bragged about his $4,500-dollar profit."

Greg pulls his handgun out of the holster. He opens the chamber assuring it's filled with rounds.

The detective closes it and lays the weapon in his lap.

A few seconds later, they pass a police squad car parked on the side of the road next to a food mart. Suddenly the vehicle's bar lights and siren turn on, and it races after them.

"We've got company, chief." Greg tells him, glancing at the car in his side mirror.

They reach the silver car, and a black Lincoln Sedan swerves from a crossroad and gets directly behind them.

Instantly, Greg looks over the back seat at it. "I think Moran's guys are on our tail." he states grabbing his revolver.

"I don't care!" Richard exclaims, "I want this son -of -a -bitch! Do me a favor, friend! Watch my back!"

"I'm on it." Greg assures him.

The detective sees another police car turning onto the road. It's nearly a block behind the other one heading their way. "We've got three on our tail now, chief." he informs him, "The Lincoln and two squad cars."

"Keep an eye on 'em!" Richard responds gunning the engine, "This bastard is not getting away! His ass is mine!"

Immediately, Greg's attention is drawn to the passenger in the dark sedan. He's extending out the window with a long, dark object in his hands.

The black car reduces its speed just as the cruisers skid to a stop.

The detective sees the man aiming at the police vehicles. "What in the hell?" Greg mumbles, puzzled.

Abruptly, he sees a flash and smoke surge in their direction on the passenger side. A huge explosion follows, flipping the squad cars off the roadway.

The detective watches the man shove the empty rocket launcher back inside the car. He sees the guy pulling out another one with a projectile attached to it. Greg observes the car's passenger maneuvering toward them with the long weapon on his shoulder. Hastily, he pats Richard on the arm. "Get off this highway, sir!" he yells looking ahead."

"What's going on!" the captain inquires.

"We've got a rocket launcher aiming at us!" the detective shouts, "Turn left on that dirt road!"

The captain trails the Mazda doing the same.

Instantly, Richard's car hydroplanes off the roadway after the maneuver.

As Captain Harris and Greg brace themselves firmly while crossing the bumpy field, they watch the lieutenant's car slam into a tree.

Richard skids into the grass and stops right beside it.

Greg gets out immediately aiming his gun towards the highway.

When the sedan turns in, he fires twice at the passenger.

The rounds struck the man's upper torso, forcing him to drop the weapon.

The Lincoln sedan slams on its brakes and slides to a halt.

Suddenly, Greg spots the driver reaching out the window. He spots a gun in the guy's hand and quickly shoots through the windshield hitting the driver.

Swiftly, he reloads and rushes around the car to check on his boss. "Chief!" he calls hurrying to his friend, "Are you alright?"

Within seconds, Greg hears traffic coming down the road at the other end. He looks immediately, spotting three more sedans heading his way. He finds Richard sitting on the ground with his back against the door. "We've gotta' get out of here sir!" he exclaims trying to help the captain to his feet.

"Forget Thompson right now!" the captain orders, "Save the girl!"

"What about you!" Greg exclaims.

"I'll be alright!" Richard says, "Don't worry about me! Just get the girl and get outta' here!"

Greg takes another glimpse at the cars coming their way on the dirt road.

Their tires are flinging dust clouds while approaching the curve.

"I'm not leaving you, sir!" he responds worrisomely, "I can't let you fight them alone!"

"He won't kill a cop right now, Greg!" the captain responds strongly, "Moran has two men in jail! I'm his bargaining tool! Rescue the girl, and get the hell outta' here! That's an order!"

"I'll find you, chief!" Greg shouts backing away, "Trust me! I'll get ya'!"

The detective dashes to Thompson's car holstering his weapon. He sees the man's head moving slowly against the driver's window, almost unconscious. Greg opens the passenger door as the hostage stares him. "Are you okay?" he asks her.

She nods and he grabs her hand. "We've gotta' get out of here." he says and the female follows him instantly.

The detective races off into the woods, pulling the young woman by the hand. He sees a downgrade leading into higher brush and takes the path in haste. The man hears the girl stumbling and turns back to assure she's alright.

Afterwards, they proceed with their rapid escape through the woods.

Chapter Eight

About twenty minutes later, Greg reaches Carlton Springs Road. He stops and releases the lady's hand, seeing no traffic at both ends of the street. "By the way, I'm Detective Hardison." he says turning to her.

"Hi." she responds, "my name is Tia Yang."

"Nice to meet you." he shakes her hand gently, both catching their breaths, "I wanna' help you."

"That man scared me." she admits with her eyes filling with tears, "I couldn't let him take my mother too. So I told him I saw the murder last night, and she was asleep. - If he's still alive, don't let him hurt me again."

"I won't let him bother you." Greg responds, "You'll be fine. Let's get you to a safe place."

"Okay." she agrees, "What about my mother and son?"

Greg pulls out his cell phone.

He grabs the lady's arm and steps back into the woods with her.

"What's wrong?" she inquires curiously.

"We've gotta' stay out of sight from the roadway." he tells her, hearing a vehicle coming up the street.

Greg dials his stepmother's house and listens for an answer.

After four rings, his wife picks up.

"Janna?" he says glancing at the light- blue truck passing by.

"Yeah, baby." she replies, "It's me. Are you okay?"

"I'm fine." Greg answers her, "Are policemen there with you?"

"Yes." Janna says, "They're outside watching the house."

"Good." he sighs in relief, "How's Landon?"

"He's okay too." she tells him, "Gary came over. He told the policemen I'll be safer over Momma's house, and they're here with us. There's another cop livin' across the street from here, but he works at night."

"That's even better." Greg states, "Where's Gary now?"

"He's in the kitchen." his wife replies, "You need to talk to him?"

"Yeah." he answers and waits for Janna to get her oldest brother to the telephone.

Shortly, Gary gets on the line. "What's goin' on, Greg?" he answers with his southern accent.

"I need a big favor." Greg says.

"Name it, man." his step brother responds.

"Go to Apartment Eight at Brookshire Apartments." he requests, "Tell Miss Yang you're helping the two nice policemen who were there, and I've got her daughter with me. Get her and the kid outta' there. Take them to your mother's house."

"You got it man." Gary agrees, "Are you okay, man?"

"I'm fine." Greg assures him, "Just do that for me and keep me up- to- date on what's happening."

"Will do man." his stepbrother agrees.

"Thanks, Gary." Greg says.

"You need to talk ta' sis again?" his stepbrother asks.

"Yeah." he replies, "Go ahead and put her on."

Greg waits a few seconds, and then she comes on the line.

"I'm here, honey." Janna tells him.

"Baby? Don't go anywhere until I get there." he says to her, "I don't want to get you and Landon any deeper in this mess. Okay?"

"I'll stay at Momma's house until you get here." She agrees, "I promise. You be careful."

"I will." the detective tells her, "I love you. And tell Landon the same."

"Okay." his wife replies, "We love you too."

They exchange goodbyes and he returns the phone to its pouch. The detective assures the Bluetooth earpiece is securely on his ear after running, and he turns to Tia. "Now let's get outta' here." Greg suggests to her.

"Okay." she answers.

Swiftly, they dash across the street to another field of woods.

The detective leads her through the brush to a narrow, winding path. He scurries down the lengthy trail with the lady closely behind him.

After going a few minutes longer, Tia is almost exhausted.

So Greg grabs her hand again and reduces his pace to a walk.

Shortly, they emerge from the path near an old wooden house. Greg sees a red semi-tractor parked on the other side of it. He stares the front door of the home while crossing the dirt road.

Mysteriously, the detective spots an old man coming out on the porch with a shotgun in his hands. So he halts instantly with Tia standing behind him.

For a few seconds, they stare each other without breathing a word.

"You two lost?" the guy asks slowly raising the weapon at them.

"No." Greg replies drawing his weapon faster than the old man's aim, "I don't want any trouble. We're just passing through."

"Fast hands." the guy comments, coming down the old wooden steps, "I can tell by the way you handle that gun, you're probably a cop."

"I am." Greg responds, "I'm Detective Hardison. If you don't mind, I've got work to do. So take the weapon back in the house, and we'll resolve this peacefully."

"Sure thing, officer." the stranger states, "I don't want any problems either."

The resident heads back up the steps with his eyes fixed on him, "Chief Harris has mentioned your name a few times." the man mentions, "He's an old friend of mine. I met him a few years ago."

"Who are you?" the detective asks, carefully lowering his aim.

"My name is Nat Devarro." the guy says, "I'm an old informant of his. How's he doing?"

"He's probably been kidnapped." Greg tells him, "We were trying to rescue this lady here. The damn lieutenant had her. I'm trying to get to a safe place."

"This doesn't have anything to do with Moran, does it?" Nat inquires standing on his porch, "If so, I can help you find him."

"How do you know that?" the detective wonders with his gun aimed at the ground.

"I used to work for Douglas." the man answers, "Who do you think I was giving the chief information about? Besides, I know Moran hates him. He wants to get rid of him. - My ex-boss set me up to take the fall for a drug heist years ago. Richard proved I had nothing to do with it. And we've been friends ever since."

"How can you help me get Captain Harris?" Greg asks.

"I still have an ole' friend in Moran's organization." Nat explains, "I know where his next big move is. It's right through those woods behind my house. Are you interested?"

"Yeah," Greg agrees, "but no tricks."

"None at all." the man assures him, "You can trust me. Your captain does. He still visits me from time to time. And Douglas thinks I'm in California in some witness protection program. He just moved part of his operation here a few years ago. So do you want my help?"

"Okay." Greg says, "Do you really think Moran took him as a hostage?"

"I'd bet my life on it." Nat agrees, "I heard about those boys of his you busted this morning. I'm sure he wants them back. – Holding Richard will be a good way ta' get 'em."

The detective holsters his weapon gazing eye to eye with the man.

Afterwards, he walks a few steps towards the porch. He gets there and halts with a short glimpse back to Tia.

Greg faces the man again with an attentive stare. "I'm listening." he says calmly to Nat, "Tell me what you know."

Chapter Nine

After Greg gets information from Nat, he proceeds on with Tia. Hastily, they rush down a wooded path behind the man's home.

The detective is thinking about what the guy told him, especially the part about the lieutenant and Commissioner Baker.

Suddenly, his cell phone rings and they stop. Greg snatches it out, and sees it's the police station's number on the caller ID. Anxiously, he answers.

"Hi. This is Tara." the caller responds, "You've got to hear what I've found out. I tried to reach Captain Harris, and only got his voice mail."

"I think he's been kidnapped." he informs her.

"By who!" she exclaims.

"I believe Moran's got something to do with it." Greg says, "Put an A. P. B. out on him. If they find him, tell them not to engage until I get there. We don't want the captain harmed. And Thompson *did* kidnap the other witness. We rescued her, and she's here with me."

"Thank God." Tara sighs. "I'll get the message out on the radio right away."

"Thanks." he tells her, "Do me a favor and find out everything you can about Thompson."

"I already have." Tara update's him, "I started on it right after you left. Our so-called *lieutenant* has a fake name." she states and goes on explaining, "I got his social security number from Human Resources. I checked his background and came up with nothing. So I traced the lieutenant's fingerprints and found out his real name is Joseph Dalton. The picture's a match. He also has a criminal record."

"Good work." the detective commends her stuffing the phone back inside the case, listening on his ear piece, "Go ahead and get the word out about the chief. I'll call you back and hear the rest shortly."

"You got it." Tara says.

Greg presses the button on his Bluetooth head device and disconnects the call. He pulls the phone back out and places it on vibrate. While returning the device to the case, the detective glances at Tia, "Let's move on." he tells her.

Again, they began to scurry down the pathway.

The pair went on nearly a hundred feet when a door slam caught their attention.

Cautiously, the detective creeps through the woods following the strange noise. He reaches the bordering tree line and views a vast open field. Greg looks closely and spots a small airstrip.

The long- paved area is parallel to the horizontal row of trees past the clearance before him.

He veers his eyes right to the old, worn warehouse with two empty docks facing him. The guy observes it in silence as most of the mysterious traffic departs.

Shortly, the man looks ahead to the back of a large trailer. It's hooked to a semi-tractor resting several feet from the warehouse door. He also notices a black sedan parked closer to him. "Nat was right." the guy utters to himself, "There is something happening here."

Abruptly, his attention is distracted by Tia sniffling behind him. So Greg looks back to her.

"Are you alright?" he asks watching her sit upon the grass.

"I'm okay." she answers.

In haste, Greg turns back to the field and stares the huge warehouse again. He draws his revolver and holds it firmly in his hand.

In that moment, the detective sees a blue-suited man coming out of the building's entrance.

The tall man emerges with another much older than him.

The elderly gentleman's wearing a cap with some dirty, denim jeans.

After exchanging words with the well-dressed man, the old guy goes to the truck.

Shortly, a third man comes outside with a very familiar face. The detective stares in sudden rage as the villain straightens his blazer. "Douglas Moran." he utters to himself.

"I don't give a damn!" he hears the man yell, "The shipment should be airlifted! The idiot should have a plane here already! This is twenty million dollars' worth of merchandise we're dealing with here!"

"Rivera's our biggest client, sir." the man wearing the blue blazer says, "You know we can't change his mind. His Florida operation is just being cautious."

"This is stupid!" Douglas replies handing his waist and stepping away, "Is he *that* scared of the Feds?" he adds turning back to his lieutenant.

"Sir?" the man speaks with hesitation, "I'm sure the shipment will get to Tampa safely, and we'll get our money."

"How in the hell do you know that Terrance!" Moran exclaims staring him angrily.

Gradually, the boss approaches the stocky, suited man. "Is there something you're not telling me, Terrance?" he asks.

"No, sir." the guy assures him, "Rivera just knows the federal agents are looking closely for the next air shipment there. They'll never expect it on the ground. We've never done that before. Besides, I've attached a G.P.S. tracking device under the truck's air tank. He can't get away."

Greg's gets frustrated. He's waiting to hear something to help him find and save Richard. "Come on." he breathes silently, continuing to listen, "Tell me what I need to know."

Douglas paces away again with a brush of the hand down his face. "You remind of Victor, my younger brother." he mentions, "That bastard pissed me off many times making arrangements like that, - without letting me know about it. – I care about him with all of my heart, but the guy is hard-headed. My brother's last solo move was his downfall. The Feds caught him and it cost him two decades in the penitentiary, with two more years left before he gets out. The court convicted him without parole. – And I don't need that misery."

Swiftly, he faces Terrance and points his index finger at him. "Don't screw this up." he blurts harshly, "I don't want any problems to lead back to me."

"Rivera's never crossed us, sir." the man tells him, "I'm sorry, but he's right this time. You have a state court date on Monday, and I believe your attorneys can get you off the hook again. All we have to do is find that damn truck driver who escaped, and the other girl who got away from Dalton. I think you and the commissioner made a big mistake hiring him anyway, - plugging him in the department as Lieutenant Thompson. He's screwing up. - I've got a dozen men on our problems right now, including that banged- up lieutenant."

"Is the Mitcham girl still in there?" Moran inquires.

"Yes sir." Terrance answers, "She's locked in the back office. I'm still skeptical about that truck driver you talked to."

Lightly, Moran shakes his head, "He wasn't desperate for money." he figures, "Stay on him. Use his family to make him talk if you need to. If the guy knows anything about our job last night, you know what to do."

"Yes sir." Terrance replies.

Strangely, Douglas appears curious. "That damn trucker *did* look familiar." he mentions, "I've seen him somewhere else. - I just can't recall where."

"Think you know him?" Terrance asks.

"I'm not sure." Moran answers, "But that's not important at this time. Where's the captain?"

"We took him to the mansion." the guy responds, "He's in the basement."

Unexpectedly, Douglas strikes Terrance in the jaw with his fist. "I told you not to take him to the house!" he reminds him bluntly, "I don't want to be tied to his kidnapping!"

Terrance tries to recover from the blow, then stands and gives him an evil look. "We tied him up and put a bag over his head!" his lieutenant blurts out, "He doesn't know where we took him!"

"I don't trust it!" the boss confesses arrogantly, "Use him to get Beck and Weaver out of jail!" Douglas decides, "Afterwards, kill him with the lieutenant's gun! Then get rid of Dalton too! Leave their bodies together in the woods, *away* from this city! - And remember to use gloves!"

"Yes sir." Terrance agrees.

Greg's still listening from the bushes. "You low- down bastard." he mumbles at Moran quietly, "You're not killing Richard." the detective adds, "Not if I can stop it."

He glances back at Tia and sees she's becoming drowsy, "I need to get you outta' here."

"I'm okay." the lady assures him, "Besides, I can use a few more minutes of rest."

The detective smiles and gives her a nod. "Okay." he voices to her softly as she grins.

Greg turns his attention back to the men at the warehouse. He veers his eyes to the elderly gentlemen wearing the worn jeans.

The old man meets Mr. Moran and Terrance with a chuckle. "You two boys wrap up your damn gossipin'." he voices bluntly, "I got a long drive ahead. Rivera's waitin' for this load."

Douglas yanks the man by the shirt and strikes him in the face. His devastating blow forces the guy to the ground. He snatches the man up and draws a handgun from his shoulder holster. The boss points it at his forehead and cocks it, "Who in the hell do you think you're talkin' to!" he groans at the trucker viciously as Terrance begs for him not to shoot the man, "I'll take this 0.44forty-four magnum and blow your damn head off! Do you understand!"

"I'm sorry!" the elderly guy shouts with blood streaming from his nostrils, "I'll never talk to ya' like that again! I promise!"

Moran pushes the man away and carefully returns the gun's hammer to its resting position. "You just make sure nothing happens to my shipment!" he shouts angrily.

"Yes sir!" the man exclaims, terrified.

"Take out your wallet!" Douglas demands harshly.

The old man stuffs his trembling hand in his rear pants pocket and pulls it out. He steps forward and hands it to him then carefully moves back.

Douglas opens it and snatches the driver's license out. He throws the wallet back in the man's chest and reads the card closely. "Is this your correct address in Tampa?" Moran inquires.

"Yeah." the man answers nervously with a nod, "I don't want any trouble, sir. I have a wife and two grown daughters at the house. I'm just out here tryin' to make a livin'."

Douglas gives him an evil look and hands him the license. "If you leak a word about anything that happened here today, I'll kill you and your whole family. Do you understand Ned?"

"Yes sir." the man acknowledges.

Douglas shifts his focus back to Terrance. "Keep him tracked." he orders, "And you stay with him until he gets to Rivera. Take a group of guys with you, and have some of my men there to join you. When the business is finished, get your ass back here."

"Yes sir." his lieutenant assures him, "The driver's leaving here at three o'clock. Rivera's expecting him at *his* warehouse in the early morning hours."

Slowly, Moran returns the large nickel-plated revolver to its holster. He looks at Ned and points his finger in his face. "The rest of the building is secured." he says, "You make sure you lock that damn lobby when you leave."

"Yes sir." the trucker agrees nervously.

Douglas lowers his arm and turns away rolling his eyes at Ned. He steps away with Terrance walking along beside him.

They're coming towards Greg, so he ducks down behind the brush peeking at them. He stays motionless until they get in the Lincoln Sedan and pull away. The detective continues watching the car until he hears it racing off on the main roadway.

Hastening, Greg returns his eyes back to the truck driver and sees him taking off his cap. Greg stares him rubbing a forearm across his nose.

Afterwards, the elderly man puts his headgear back on and heads back into the warehouse.

The detective looks around and spots a vast field of grass on the opposite side of the airfield. He sees a tall sign behind the bordering trees reading "The Food Palace." The man gives it a short stare. "I know where we are." he remembers.

The guy gives one more glimpse to the tractor and trailer then looks at his watch. "One o'clock." he breathes lightly to himself, "I've got an idea."

The officer pulls out his phone again. He calls his stepmother's house and waits for an answer.

After a few rings, someone picks up the line. "Hello." the guy says with a familiar voice.

"Gary?" Greg calls.

"Yeah. This is me, man." his stepbrother responds.

"Did you get the lady and her grandson?" the detective wonders.

"Sure did." Gary acknowledges.

"Good." he says, "I need one more favor. Can you pick up her daughter in front of The Food Palace in twenty minutes."

"Okay." his stepbrother agrees.

"If she's not there, wait for her." the officer says, "She looks just like her mother - slim with long, dark hair - wearing a light- blue top and white sweat pants."

"Got it." Gary states, "I'll be there."

"Thanks." Greg voices, "I owe you man."

"You don't owe me anything." his stepbrother tells him, "If you need something else, just let me know."

"I appreciate it man." the detective expresses and ends the call.

Greg returns the phone to its pouch with a short sigh. He turns back to Tia. "Come here." the officer asks her and she approaches him, "You see that sign right there?" the guy inquires, pointing to it.

"Yes." she answers, looking with him.

"In about twenty minutes, -" he pauses, placing a hand upon her shoulder, "I want you to go to that building right below that sign. Look for a little red truck. And he'll take you to your mother and son, okay?"

"Alright." Tia responds.

"We have to wait a few minutes." he hesitates, explaining, "I've got to make sure nobody's in that warehouse except that little old man, got it?"

The lady nods with a smile.

Chapter Ten

About fifteen minutes have passed. Greg sends Tia across the field heading to the restaurant.

Once she gets out of sight, the detective raises his weapon and faces the warehouse. He steps out of the brush and heads for the tractor and trailer. Greg creeps towards it aiming the handgun at the warehouse door.

Moving closer, he hears the truck's engine idling.

The detective reaches the driver's side and races to the truck door holstering his weapon.

Quickly, he feels under the air tanks and wraps his hand around the tracking device. He yanks it off and throws it into the woods.

Cautiously, Greg opens the door to the cab and climbs in. He closes the door quietly and pushes the brake knobs in.

The detective steps on the clutch and shifts to fourth gear.

Very gently, he eases off the clutch and the vehicle begins rolling.

Swiftly, Greg steers to the left turning the rig around. He makes a complete circle and faces the dirt road.

The guy straightens the tractor and trailer while looking in the driver side mirror. He sees no sign of the little old man, and creeps on down the path.

Shortly, Greg gets to the main roadway and spots a sign reading Highway 51. So he makes a wide turn to the left and heads away from the city.

The detective releases a sigh of relief while attaching his seat belt. Hastening, he looks in the truck's mirrors again. He sees it's clear for the moment and accelerates rapidly.

After up-shifting to the tenth gear, Greg's cell phone vibrates. He presses the button on his earpiece and answers the call.

"This is Gary." his stepbrother tells him, "I got the lady with me."

"Thanks." Greg says.

"Don't worry about it, man." Gary advises him, "She's safe. Call me if you need me."

"Okay." the detective assures him.

After disconnecting the call, the guy pulls his phone out and carefully scrolls to a friend's number with his thumb. He makes the call and listens for a ring.

"Hello." a man answers.

"Henry?" Greg asks, "Is that you?"

"Yeah, man." his friend recognizes his voice, "What's going on? I'm glad to hear from ya. I thought you'd probably be on the road right now."

"Really, I am." Greg responds returning the phone to its case, "Have you got any space in that big ole' barn of yours?"

"Yeah." Henry replies with a pause, "What ya' need it for?"

"I need to park an eighteen- wheeler in it." Greg tells him, "Can you do that for me?"

"No problem, man." Henry agrees, "I think I still owe ya' about a hundred dollars anyway."

The detective giggles. "We'll call it even." he settles with him, "You want me to come in on the Deer Creek side?"

"That'll be fine." his friend agrees, "How long will it be before ya' get' here?"

"About twenty to thirty minutes." Greg replies, "I'm coming south down Highway 51 now. I'll intersect with Deer Creek Road in less than ten minutes."

"Alright." Henry says, "I'll go and open the gate for ya'."

"Thanks." he tells his friend.

"No sweat, man." Henry utters kindly, "I'll see ya' in a few minutes."

The detective disconnects the call and checks his mirrors again. He still sees it clear of traffic and returns his eyes to the roadway.

A few seconds later, Greg glances aside and sees Ned's cell phone in the passenger seat.

The mobile unit is attached to a charger with a long cord, displaying two missed calls.

The detective leans over to it and wraps his hand around the piece. He picks it up and scrolls through the contact numbers. "Come on." he mumbles to himself, "There's got to be some number I can use."

Eventually, the guy finds Douglas Moran's number in the directory. "That's good enough for me." he says.

So Greg closes the flip phone and snatches it away from the charger cord. He stuffs it inside his blazer pocket and races on down the highway.

Mysteriously, the guy spots someone standing in the middle of the roadway.

At this distance, Greg can see it's a Caucasian girl with long brown hair. He stares the blue and gray jacket as she continues running towards him.

Drastically, the man brakes and steers to the shoulder.

He stops and shifts to neutral. The guy pulls out the brake knobs just as the girl opens the passenger door. "Get in!" the detective shouts to her over the engine noise.

The female climbs in the truck and gets in the passenger seat. She shuts the door breathing heavily and gasping for air.

Immediately, Greg gets the truck on the roadway again. He builds up his speed and levels at seventy miles per hour.

The man glances at the young lady. "Put your seat belt on." he asks, and she does.

He looks in the side mirrors again and returns his eyes to the highway. "Are you Kera Mitcham?" the guy asks.

"Yes." she answers sniffling.

"I'm Detective Hardison." he introduces himself and hesitates, "I was in the truck yard last night when Cole got shot." he admits, "I'm sorry you had to see that. I'll do what I can to help you. We'll see that the killer pays for what he's done."

"Thank you." she sighs with watery eyes.

"Are you alright?" Greg asks.

"Yes." Kera answers, "I'm just hungry."

"We'll get you something to eat." he assures her, "How did you get away?"

"When the guard escorted me to the restroom, I found a box cutter blade on the floor." she confesses in a breath, "I picked it up when he wasn't looking and cuffed it in my hands. The guy waited for me to get done and he tied my hands again. He took me back to the office with a window. The man left and locked the door. That's when I cut the rope and climbed out to get away."

Greg looks at her with a warm grin and nods. "You did the right thing." he commends her, "Smart thinking."

Gradually, the detective moves his eyes back to the highway. "You're safe now." he assures her, "I'll get you home."

Chapter Eleven

Minutes later, Greg arrives at Henry's gate leading to the huge barn. His friend waves and stands aside as he pulls in.

Greg steers wide to fit the semi-tractor and trailer inside. He looks in his driver mirror and sees the fifty - three feet van barely missing the fence pole.

The detective clears the entrance and pulls into the dirt road heading towards the building.

Greg gives a glimpse to Kera. "This man is my friend." he mentions, "I'll borrow one of his trucks to get you home."

"Okay." she agrees, "Thank you."

"You're welcome." he acknowledges.

The detective reaches the barn and pulls all the way inside.

Afterwards, he shifts to neutral and pulls out the brake knobs. "It's okay to get out now." he says to her. Greg powers down the truck and climbs out. He closes the door and walks to rear of the vehicle. The man glances at the padlock on the trailer doors and continues on to meet Henry.

"You can't move no faster than that old man!" Greg yells to him grinning.

Henry looks at him with a short giggle. "I've been cuttin' grass all day!" he responds adjusting his ball cap, "I'm a retired old man! I ain't gotta' hurry for nothin'! I let you young bucks handle it these days! Now, go get me a sausage and biscuit! - And a cup of coffee!"

Both of them burst in laughter and shake hands once they meet.

"What's up, old friend?" Henry asks releasing his handshake.

"Quite a bit, man." Greg tells him, gradually dropping his smile, "We've got a lot to talk about."

"You ain't dressed like no trucker." his friend says.

"I'm back on the force now." the detective admits, "We've got a hot twenty-million- dollar shipment here. We've gotta' close these doors."

"Sure thing, man." his friend agrees and heads first to the huge front doors.

Greg does the same to the back doors and returns to meet his friend.

"I can see this ain't your rig." Henry mentions and stops a few feet before him.

"No." Greg answers, "I stole it."

His friend shortly laughs and steps forward giving him a pat on the shoulder. "I know Richard leaped plum outta' his chair when you came back." he says, "You answered his prayer, man. - That's all he talked about to me, - was gettin' you back workin' for him again."

Greg bows his head sadly and steps away noticing Kera sitting on a bale of hay.

"What's wrong, man?" Henry asks, "You know I'll help you anyway I can. We're friends and worked together for years in that police department. We'll figure this one out."

The detective turns back to him. "The captain's been kidnapped." he states.

"What!" Henry exclaims, slowly approaching him, "How did that happen?"

Suddenly, Greg's cell phone rings.

"You go ahead and take that call." his friend advises and paces away, "It might be important."

"Hello?" the detective answers.

"What's up, bro?" the familiar voice asks happily.

"How's it goin', Wade?" he responds.

"I'm doing fine, man," his older brother replies, "Tell me something new."

"You don't wanna' know." Greg pauses, "There's a lot happening here."

"Momma and Daddy said hi, and to take care of yourself." Wade informs him, "You've got me worried about you now."

"Unfortunately, -" the detective expresses with hesitation, "Captain Harris has been kidnapped."

"How did that happen?" Wade asks, concerned.

Greg glances at Henry introducing himself to Kera. He takes a deep breath and proceeds with the call. "We were tailing his lieutenant." Greg hesitates and continues explaining, "The man kidnapped a witness to a murder. - Miss Nora's son was shot and killed last night."

"Cole!" his brother exclaims.

"Yeah." Greg says, "I saw Moran shoot him in the head with my own eyes."

"Douglas Moran?" Wade wonders.

"That's him." the detective admits.

"He won a federal case here in Tampa about six months ago." his brother informs him and pauses, "We had him, man. Those damn lawyers from Miami got him acquitted on all charges, - arms smuggling, murder, and drugs. The witnesses wouldn't testify or disappeared. The court couldn't place him at the scene of the crimes."

"He's got a court case here Monday." Greg tells him, "The witnesses are also having a problem here, including me."

"Do you know if he's doing any business there?" Wade inquires.

"Yes." the detective answers, "He was selling a shipment today to a guy named Rivera in your city, – until I stopped it."

"Are you back on the police force again?" his brother asks.

"Yeah." Greg replies, "Rivera's shipment won't make it to Florida tonight."

"I know who he is." his brother recalls, "I'll get the bureau to open an investigation on it right now. We'll join forces with our F.B.I. branch there. Stand by for my call. I'm flying there tonight."

"Got it." Greg states, "Be careful."

"You do the same." Wade responds.

They exchange goodbyes and the detective ends the call.

He spots Henry kneeling down at the front tire on the passenger's side of the tractor. His friend is grabbing something on the inner frame above it.

The detective creeps toward him curiously and squats to see what Henry's looking at.

"I'll be damned." his friend mumbles and turns to him with a puzzled look upon his face, "You gotta' pocket knife?" the man asks holding out his hand.

"Yeah." Greg answers, digging inside his pocket to retrieve it.

The detective gives it to him, and Henry uses the tool to pry something away from the underbody.

Greg waits a moment and watches him turn around with a device like a quarter-size watch battery.

He doesn't see any wires attached to it, only a dry glue substance.

Gradually, Henry holds it up observing it. "This is a tracking device?" he says, "I used these things years ago to solve quite a few cases, remember?"

"Yeah." Greg looks at it closer with him. "That's probably Rivera's GPS unit." he replies, "I threw away Moran's when I stole the truck."

"I figured they had a way of following it." his friend adds, "Twenty million dollars is a lot of money."

"I gotta' get rid of it." the detective decides, "We can't let them track it here. I hope he hasn't talked to Rivera yet."

"I'm sure he will." Henry agrees standing with the device, "I think you better get this thing outta' here."

"Can I use one of your trucks?" Greg asks taking the piece from him, "My car is still at the police station."

"Yeah." his friend says pointing to the back, "Take that blue Ford out there. I think the key is still in it."

"Thanks man." the detective responds and points to Kera with a glimpse, "I'll go ahead and get her home?"

"Alright." Henry answers, "Call if you need me."

"Thanks." Greg tells him and heads for the back doors with the girl, "I'll get back as soon as I can."

"Take your time." Henry advises him.

The detective leaves the barn and goes to the truck by the tractor. On the way, he notices Kera looking around strangely.

"He owns all of these vehicles?" she asks.

"Every one of them." the detective replies with a snicker, "Give him time. He'll have more than this."

Both of them glance at each other with a grin.

Chapter Twelve

Greg's made it back to Highway 51, returning to the city area. He checks his watch and sees it's almost three o'clock. The detective's approaching the dirt road to the airfield. So he accelerates to pass it.

Just as the man goes by, he looks in the rear view mirror and sees it's clear for now.

So the detective rolls down his window. He pulls out the tracking device Henry gave him and tosses it out on the pavement.

Suddenly, he spots a convoy of black automobiles heading towards him. The cars are on the other side of the road traveling like they're going to a funeral. The guy knows the nearest intersecting road is about a mile ahead. So he remains calm and continues cruising in the pickup. Greg's not worried much for himself. It's Kera he's concerned about right now. The man gives her a glimpse. "Put your head down for a moment." he requests and she proceeds to do so.

Within seconds, the Lincoln sedans approach and pass them.

The man gazes in the rear view mirror again, making sure they keep going.

He glances over to Kera. "You can get up now." he informs her, "It's okay."

As she rises in her seat, Greg gazes ahead to a lonely highway. He drifts into a thought, remembering a troubling night just over three years ago.

About ten p. m. on a Thursday, the detective enters the police station looking for an old college classmate named Karen Flannigan.

She'd called him earlier, arranging to meet him to discuss an urgent matter. They sat down at his desk, briefly discussing their past times as college students. Afterwards, she grew sad and tearful for some reason. Just as the lady begins talking, she shifts her eyes to the hallway on the left.

She becomes terrified instantly.

Greg looks, and no one's standing there but a brown-bearded white man wearing a tan trench coat.

Immediately, Karen says she has to go. She gets up and rushes for the double- glass doors to exit the building.

The detective hurries after her, but she's gotten farther ahead of him. He emerges from the precinct and tries to catch her before she pulls away. Greg misses a step and stumbles to the pavement.

Karen fish-tails the car and almost hits him driving off.

His co-worker, Rhonda, arrives in her squad car just as it happens. She must think it's a hit and run accident. So the female detective storms after the vehicle, balling her tires.

The man dashes to his personal automobile in the lot and hurries to follow them. He loses sight of them and calls Rhonda from his cell phone. The guy gets no answer. So Greg tries to reach Karen.

After three rings, she picks up. "Help me!" she exclaims desperately, "He's gonna' kill me!"

"Who!" the man asks, confused.

"My boyfriend!" Karen replies, "I found out how he murdered his wife! His guys are stalking me everywhere!"

"Where are you?" the detective responds worrisomely.

"I'm on Taylor Bend Road!" she implies, "I'm passing a lumber company!"

"I know where you are." he recognizes the area, "I'm on my way."

Greg stomps the gas pedal and fishtails while making a right turn. He straightens the car on the roadway and races toward the outskirts.

Minutes later, the detective is storming down Taylor Bend Road. He's on a long stretch about two miles from the city limits. He sees no trace of Karen *or* Rhonda.

Shortly, he notices three pairs of taillights in the distance. One set is on a vehicle with a bright police bar light on top. The other lamps are on cars parked in the grass, near the wood line. He sees two people scuffling in the grass. Looking left in the moon's bright glow, Greg spots Karen stumbling while running to the woods.

She appears to be escaping from the scene.

Swiftly, he draws his revolver and lays it upon the seat. The man's close enough now and sees Rhonda fighting a dark-masked man subdued in black. So he steers to the shoulder and slams on the brakes. Just as Greg skids, he hears a gunshot. The guy observes Rhonda falling to the ground.

Hastening, Detective Hardison spots the attacker rushing to the woods also. He snatches his weapon from the seat and flings the car door open. The man gets out quickly staring Rhonda's motionless body.

Afterward, he turns his eyes to the masked stranger and sees a gun aimed at him. The detective ducks down by the car tire as the assailant fires twice. As Greg peeks over the hood, he witnesses Karen being shot in the back by the stalker.

The shooter faces him again and fires three more times striking the pavement aside.

Swiftly, Greg locks an aim with his arms on the hood. He shoots at the attacker six times and watches him stagger into the woods. The detective reloads and closes the chamber to his weapon. He races to the trees with a tactical aim, carefully scanning his eyes for the man. Greg creeps into the woods, surrounded by a sudden silence. Abruptly, the guy gets a glimpse of the suspect's silhouette. So he fires three more rounds at the figure before it vanishes between the trees.

Quickly, the detective shifts his locked aim to the left hand. He backs away slowly, reaching for his phone with the other hand to call for help.

Suddenly, Greg's startled from his daze by a loud semi-truck horn. He steers right off the yellow line in haste as the vehicle passes beside him.

The detective glances at Kera and moves his eyes back to the roadway. "Sorry." he apologizes to her.

"You've had a hard day like me." she says with a smile.

Greg gives her a short grin and returns his focus to the view ahead. He pulls out his cell phone and calls the police dispatcher. After a couple of rings, someone answers. "Redwood Springs Police Department." he hears, "May I help you?"

"Sergeant Maddox?" the detective says recognizing her voice.

"Hey, Greg." she responds, "What's going on?"

"Can you get some squad cars to the Mitcham residence." he requests, "I've got Kera with me, and I don't want her family harmed. The kidnappers are still at large."

"I'll get right on it." the sergeant assures him, "I'll send two over there right now."

"Patricia." the man adds, "If they need anything, have our guys to take care of them. I don't want Kera and her family leaving the house tonight. — When Moran notices she's gone, I believe he'll do anything to get her."

"They'll be in good hands." she states, "*You* be careful."

"I will." he tells her, "Thanks."

"We've heard nothing about the captain yet." Sergeant Maddox informs him, "I'll call you as soon as we find out anything."

"I'll get him." the detective voices calmly, "Just get a team ready to move in."

"You got it." she replies, "Take care."

"You too." Greg tells her and ends the call.

The man puts the phone away and looks ahead as they approach the city area. He spots a fast- food restaurant on his left by a strip mall. "Do you want a burger and fries?" he asks giving Kera a glimpse, "I'm buying."

The girl nods and smiles. "Thanks." she says.

"You're welcome." he responds signaling to turn into the parking lot.

Chapter Thirteen

Greg's left the Mitcham residence and looks at his watch. He sees it's almost four o'clock in the evening. The guy's approaching Eighth Avenue and decides to take a chance with going home. So he turns left heading towards Ralston Avenue.

Within a few minutes, the detective reaches the street. He makes the turn and proceeds towards the house cautiously.

The man gazes ahead, seeing only familiar vehicles in the neighborhood.

Shortly, he arrives at his driveway and pulls in behind his wife's car. The guy shifts to park and shuts down the engine.

Hastening, Greg gets out and heads for the front door. He pulls his key ring from his pants pocket and fingers through them.

The man finds the one to get inside and unlocks the door quickly.

He gives another glimpse to the street and hurries into the house.

The detective secures the front door and runs down the hallway. He gets to the bedroom and takes his shoes off. The guy scurries removing his suit and tosses it on the bed with the keys and badge. He unloosens the tie and pulls it over his head. Greg throws it on the bed and takes off his shoulder holster.

After tossing his strapped revolver on the mattress, he hurries to the closet. The man snatches the door open and yanks a pair of black trousers off the hanger. He puts them on and gets a shirt the same color.

After shoving his arms into the sleeves, the detective pulls his black wooden chest out of the closet. He rushes back to the bed and puts on the shoulder holster.

Greg walks to the bedroom window and glances outside. The man sees it's still clear, so he rushes back to his hangers and snatches a matching jacket out. The detective puts it on and folds down the collar.

Quickly, he dashes back to the bed and stuffs his badge inside the jacket pocket. The guy grabs his key ring and fingers through them again. The detective finds the one for the padlock securing the chest. He rushes to the wooden box and opens it haste, then drops the key ring to the carpet. Instantly, he goes through the contents. Greg pulls out his Norinco SKS rifle. He sees it still has an empty, fixed ten-round magazine attached. So he flips the weapon upside down and rests the top upon the carpet. The man scurries to the bedroom closet again. He gets a standard flat- tip Phillips screwdriver and hurries back to the rifle. Quickly, Greg pushes his left palm down on trigger assembly's bottom. He uses the other hand to push the locking pin with the tool. After the guy applies force, the spring releases the assembly. He pulls the unit out and lays it on the carpet. Greg snatches the fixed magazine out and places that aside too. The detective reinstalls the trigger mechanism and assures it's locked in place. He lifts his black bag from the chest. The man unzips the garment and pulls a loaded thirty- round magazine out of it. He inserts the item in the open slot of the rifle.

Hastening, Greg checks the bag for additional ammo and magazines for the weapon. He does the same for the nine- millimeter handgun tucked under his stocking cap. The man stuffs two extra boxes of rounds and another loaded rifle magazine inside the garment bag. He tosses the screwdriver and empty fixed magazine in the bottom of the black chest.

Still hurrying, the detective secures the storage box and returns it to the closet.

After shutting the door, the man rushes for his black combat boots under the bed. He sits down and puts them on, then ties the strings firmly.

The guy gets up and slings the bag across his body. He picks up the rifle and does the same with it.

The man returns to the bed and pulls Ned's cell phone and the magnum rounds from his blazer. He shoves them inside his jacket pockets and glances at his watch.

After making sure he has *his* cell phone, the guy looks around to see what else he needs to do.

Abruptly, the detective retrieves his keys from the floor. He gives a pat to his holstered revolver and rushes back to the living room.

When Greg enters the area, he goes to the curtains and peeks outside. He sees no one outside right now, not even neighbors. So the man rushes to the front door and goes out in a hurry. He secures the knob and deadbolt.

Immediately, the detective dashes for the truck.

After reaching the vehicle, the guy snatches the door open. He removes the rifle and props it up against the passenger door. The man throws the bag in the seat on that side and gets in himself.

Quickly, the detective starts the truck. He shifts it in reverse and backs out facing Eighth Avenue. The guy looks around a final time, shoving the gear in drive.

Immediately, Greg accelerates and races away.

Chapter Fourteen

Nearly twenty minutes later, Greg turns south on Highway 51 heading back to Henry's place.

The man reaches inside his jacket pocket and pulls out Ned's phone. He thumbs through the directory until Douglas's number is displayed. The detective calls the man and swaps hands on the steering wheel. He holds it up to his left ear and listens for it to ring.

It sounds twice, and someone answers.

"Ned! Where in the hell are you!" the mob boss shouts angrily.

"He's probably looking for your ass, bastard!" the detective yells back, "Here's the deal! You've got a shipment ripped off! I can dump it in the river right now! So how bad do you want this merchandise back!"

"Who in the hell is this!" Moran exclaims angrily.

"I asked you a damn question!" Greg screams, "I'll tell you what! I'll start dumping your goods until you decide to answer! Tell me when to stop!"

"Alright!" Douglas blurts worrisomely, suddenly willing to comply, "What in the hell do you want!"

"This is the damn plan, hotshot!" the detective begins explaining, "You get one half of the shipment once you safely release the captain! I just got outta' the pen! I've got an old score to settle wit' him!"

"When do we meet!" Moran asks harshly.

"Wait on my next phone call! Then you'll know when and where!" Greg replies bluntly, "Let me talk to Captain Harris!"

"He's not at this location." the mob boss responds.

"I know you're lying, Douglas!" the detective disagrees, "Put him on the line or some of this expensive garbage is going swimming!"

"Damnit! Hold on a moment!" Moran answers frustrated, "I'll let you talk to him! Just hang on!"

"Don't put him on speakerphone!" Greg yells, "This is none of your damn business! If anybody's gonna' kill Harris, it'll be me!"

Greg hears him order someone to untie the captain, and he waits patiently for Richard to come on the line. In less than a minute, the chief answers.

"Hello." Richard says.

"Sir?" the detective speaks with a pause, "Just give me yes or no answers. Are you alright?"

"Yes." The captain replies.

"I'll have a squad car to pick you up at the drop point." he informs him, "Just cooperate with me right now. My name is Albert Jackson. You busted me six years ago for drug trafficking. You confiscated one hundred thousand dollars from me, and I served ten years in the state penitentiary. Now, I want my money back. Got that?"

"Yes." Captain Harris agrees.

"Now put that bastard back on the line." the detective requests, and he does so.

Moran returns to the phone. "Yeah." he answers with a grumpy voice.

"No tricks, Douglas!" Greg emphasizes.

"I have some questions for you!" Moran blurts out irately, "How do you know my name? And how did you know about that trailer?"

"Your damn driver left the phone in the truck!" Detective Hardison replies, "I called the first bastard in his directory - which happens to be you! As for your driver! He's like everyone else! Anyone will talk with a loaded gun in their face! - One of your men is side-steppin' ya'! He sold one of my boys some goods from you'! He said you're the man! I know your stash is in the warehouse!"

"What about Harris!" the boss shouts, "How did you know he was here?"

"I followed the son -of -a -bitch this afternoon!" Greg answers, "Your men took him! And I trailed them! So much for the damn questions! Just answer the phone when I call back!"

"I don't even know if I can trust you!" the boss exclaims.

"Think about the shipment!" the detective says with arrogance, "If you want to see it again, don't screw up! I'll call you back in a few hours!"

The detective disconnects the call and returns the phone to his pocket. He retrieves *his* from the case and dials the police station's number.

"Redwood Springs Police Department," Sergeant Maddox answers. "Can I help you?"

"This is Greg, Patricia." the officer states, "I'm gonna' need help to rescue the captain later."

"You need the S. W. A. T. team?" she inquires.

"Not yet." the man responds, "Just two officers and a squad car will do."

"I'll bring Frank with me." she suggests, "We'll take care of it."

"Okay." he agrees, "I'll call you back later with the plan. How late are you working?"

"We'll be here 'till midnight." Patricia informs him, "Unless I have to do overtime."

"Good." the detective says, "Thanks."

"You're welcome." the sergeant assures him, "Talk to ya' later."

"Alright." he tells her and ends the call.

Greg puts his phone away and readjusts the earpiece on the right ear. Just as he does, a phone call comes through with a ring. The detective presses the answer button on his headpiece. "Hello?' he says passing a slow-moving car.

"Detective Hardison?" the male speaks with a calm voice.

"Yes." Greg utters returning to his lane.

"I'm Robert Wilkins with Internal Affairs." the man introduces himself, "How are you doing today?"

Greg hesitates, skeptical. "I'm alright." he replies a little slow, "How can I help you?"

"I need to ask you some questions." the man adds, "I spoke with one of your coworkers earlier. She told me some disturbing information about Lieutenant Thompson. So I'm launching a confidential investigation and I need your help."

"What is her name?" the detective inquires, cautious.

"Tara Spencer," Robert says, "from the Special Investigations Department."

"Okay." Greg recalls the conversation with her, "What do you need to know?"

"She said Alvin might be involved with Captain Harris's kidnapping." the guy mentions, "Are you aware of that?"

"Can I trust you?" the detective asks.

"Of course." Mr. Wilkins responds, "If you give me some hard evidence, I'll proceed with an arrest warrant right now."

Greg gives a brief sigh. "The captain and I both know he assaulted and kidnapped a young woman." he testifies, "That's why we were chasing Thompson this morning. I believe he was taking her to Moran."

"You mean Douglas Moran?" Mr. Wilkins asks.

"Yes." the detective answers.

"He has a grand jury trial here Monday." Robert remembers, "He's out on one million dollars' bail. If Moran's involved, I can get that revoked."

"Hold on a minute, sir." Greg requests, "You can have the lieutenant. But leave Douglas alone until I get the captain."

"You can't take him down by yourself." the director blurts out, suddenly agitated, "He's got an entire organization backing him up. Besides, I don't want him to leave the city before his trial. Those damn lawyers of his have got their way with the system. They convinced the judge he's not a flight risk. I think he is."

"Listen, sir." the detective interrupts him, "He's not going anywhere."

"How do you know that?" Robert asks bluntly.

"Just trust me, sir." Greg demands, "The man is not leaving this city. I've got something he wants desperately. The merchandise belongs to him, and it will definitely help us put him away for good. I can promise you that. If it fails, you can have my badge. – We'll get the captain back tonight. You have my word on it."

"What do you have?" Mr. Wilkins inquires, curious.

"Please." the detective begs, "Just trust me right now. You won't be disappointed, - and keep this between *us*."

Robert becomes silent.

Greg hesitates too, wordless.

"And you don't need backup?" Mr. Wilkins asks, "I really don't think you should go in without it."

"No sir." Greg assures him, "I've got this."

"Okay." the director approves, "You've got twenty-four hours. If you don't succeed, I'll get a warrant and we'll move in.

"Fair enough, sir." the detective agrees.

After exchanging goodbyes, Greg disconnects the call. He shakes his head lightly a couple of times. "Damn." he mumbles to himself, "That was a close one."

The detective looks ahead and sees he's approaching his turn. He's chooses the street about a mile before the airfield. The guy slows down rapidly before reaching the intersection.

Suddenly, Greg has a strong urge to use the restroom. He starts squirming in his seat, staring the food mart on the corner.

Rapidly, the man steers into the lot. He pulls on the side of the building and brakes hard to stop. Hastening, Greg shoves the truck in park. He shuts the engine off and rushes out of the vehicle.

The guy slams the door and hurries to the store's entrance.

He goes inside quickly and the cashier looks at him.

Instantly, Greg points to the back while passing.

The female behind the counter nods and gives him a grin.

A couple of minutes later, Greg comes out of the restroom. He breathes a sigh of relief while gazing at the hot dog rack.

The detective strolls to the cooler and retrieves a sixteen- ounce drink.

After doing so, he looks aside and notices a male customer approaching the counter. He listens to the stocky, red-haired guy complain about a gas pump.

As Greg moves on for his hot dogs, the angry man gets louder. So he continues observing while the guy argues at the cashier.

The lady politely suggests for him to move to another pump, but he refuses.

The detective looks through the glass door at the entrance and spots a pickup attached to a horse trailer. He sees it parked at the pump the man has a problem with.

Eventually, the cashier convinces him to pull to the fuel lane on the left.

The customer storms out the double glass doors, flinging both of them open.

The woman shrugs her shoulders as Greg steps to the counter. She rings him up on the register and takes his money.

After completing the transaction, the female bags his items.

The detective gives a glimpse outside again and spots two black Lincoln sedans pulling into the fuel island. He turns his eyes to a third black Continental stopping at the pump the irate man was assigned.

The red-haired guy is blocked and can't move into the lane. So he gets out of his truck to confront the driver of the Lincoln.

Greg continues watching from the counter and notices Terrance emerging from the car. He grabs his bag and creeps aside to the body-size stand-up poster.

There, the detective proceeds to watch the scene.

The other two pairs of men emerge from their sedans. They begin to close in on the stranger approaching.

Terrance is facing the customer and slowly opens one side of his blazer.

The red-haired man halts and holds his palms out before him. He starts backing away cautiously as the other crew members lock their eyes upon him.

Greg glances at the cashier. "Have those guys been here before?" he asks.

"Yes." she answers, "Several times."

"Have they ever threatened you?" he inquires.

"Not yet." the lady responds, "They're usually stone-faced and blunt. The men get what they want and move on."

The man shows her his badge. "I'm Detective Hardison." he introduces himself, "If you feel safe with them, I'll leave."

"Thanks." the cashier says, "You can go on. I believe I'll be alright."

"Okay." he says watching the crew coming toward the entrance, "I need to go out the back way. I've gotta' confront these guys sometime. But if you don't feel safe, I'll stay."

"I'll be fine." she responds handing him the bag, "Go ahead. I'll lock it up after they leave."

Greg stuffs the badge back inside his pocket and scurries to the rear of the store. He dashes out the back exit and shuts the metal door.

Carefully, the detective peeks around the building.

He sees the area is safe now. So the man dashes to the truck. He gets inside quickly and fits his bag in the seat. The guy slams the door, rattling the window.

Hastening, Greg glances around while starting the engine.

After seeing the coast is clear, he shifts to reverse and floors the gas pedal.

The man backs out quickly, facing away from the intersection.

Immediately, he shifts to drive and races down the side street.

Chapter Fifteen

Greg arrives at Henry's barn and pulls in front of the gates. He gets out and opens them quickly then runs back to the truck.

The detective drives inside and sees his friend opening a barn door for him.

Hastily, the guy steps out of the truck. "Leave it closed!" he yells to him, "I'll come around back!"

Instantly, Greg shuts the gates and returns to the vehicle. He moves on to the rear of the building and pulls by the first barn door.

Suddenly, the detective spots Henry's brown dog racing towards him from the house. The man giggles while watching him, seeing the little dust clouds from its feet.

As Greg shuts down the engine, the animal reaches the door. He stays in a moment as the dog paws the window.

"Get down, Patch!" Henry orders his pet, and the dog runs to him. "She ain't gonna' bother ya'." his friend says to him.

The detective rolls down the window and holds his arm out with a smile.

Happily, the dog returns to him wagging its tail.

Patch sniffs his hand and runs back to Henry.

"Sorry about opening the front door, man." his friend says.

"That's alright." Greg responds, "I just don't want to cause you any trouble out here."

"I understand." Henry tells him, "Did ya' get rid of that tracking device?"

"Yeah." he answers as they step inside the barn, "And the bait's been swallowed."

"What did you do?" his friend asks halting, handing his waist.

"Moran knows I have it." the detective admits pointing at the trailer, "He doesn't know it's me yet. I told Richard to give him my fake name."

"How did ya' get in touch with him?" Henry inquires.

Greg faces him. "The truck driver left his phone in the seat." he explains, "Moran's number was in it. - I made a deal with him. I'm exchanging one half of the shipment for Richard."

"And the other?" Henry wonders.

"I'll figure that out later." the detective replies turning to the trailer, "Now let's see what's in this thing. Do you have bolt cutters and a crow bar around here?"

"Yeah." Henry answers pointing to an old tool box beside his planks of wood, "There's a good size pair of cutters over there. The crow bar is behind your trailer."

"Good." Greg responds walking to the rear of the trailer, "Let's get busy."

"Sounds good to me." Henry agrees and heads toward his stack of lumber, "I'll turn my flood lights on in here too. It'll give us more light."

The detective walks to the other side of the trailer.

When Henry illuminates the area, he picks up the steel bar near the garden tools.

Greg spots a flashlight lying aside. So he picks it up to see if it works.

The man turns the light on and off then shoves the item inside his pocket.

After doing so, the guy hears Henry talking to a young man. He recognizes the voice and strolls to the front of the semi-tractor.

When Greg gets there, he's greeted by his friend's son. "Nice to see you again, Tommy." he shakes the son's hand as Henry returns, "You've grown up and look just like your popular daddy."

His friend snickers handing him the bolt cutters. "Hell, I ain't nobody." the guy tells him, "I'm just an old white man tryin' to make a dollar."

The three of them chuckle briefly, and Greg pats his friend's upper arm.

Tommy starts to turn away, and the detective stops him with a shoulder tap.

The detective looks at him with a smile. "Can you do me a favor?" he requests, "Since you're over twenty-one now, I can't talk to you like a kid anymore."

"Sure." the son agrees, "What do you need, sir."

"Even though you're a grown man," Greg pauses and points to Henry, "always take advice from your father." he recommends, "This guy is one the wisest men I've ever met - and a best friend."

"I will." Tommy assures him.

The detective looks at Henry. "Can you get my rifle and bag out of the truck?" he asks, "I'm going to open this trailer so we can check it out. - I'll throw my trash away in a few minutes. I bought some hot dogs and a drink."

"No problem." his friend says, "I'll get ''em."

"Thanks." Greg tells him.

As Henry and his son step away, the detective cuts the lock. He throws the stray pieces aside and opens the trailer doors.

Greg rests the bar upon van's floor and carefully climbs inside.

Once the man stands, he wraps his hand around the head of the flashlight. The detective pulls it out of his back pocket and turns the item on. He shines the beam ahead and hesitates staring the contents.

Shortly, Greg reaches down and picks up the bar. He steps between a small aisle in the middle of the wooden crates. He sees fifteen large crates on each side. They're just over three feet high, all positioned evenly.

The detective reaches the nose of the trailer. He lays the flashlight down on the box beside him. The guy points the beam to the first on his left and lifts the crow bar in his other hand.

Forcefully, Greg opens the nailed wooden top with the flat part of the tool.

Afterwards, the detective rests the bar on the crate to his right. He looks back to the one he'd opened.

Carefully, Greg lifts the top off. He places it on the wooden box behind it. The man reaches for the flashlight and shines it on the contents. The detective sees stacks of clear bags containing a white powder substance. He grabs one with his other hand and heads back to the rear of the trailer.

Greg gets there and kneels down. He shuts off the flashlight and lays the bag on the trailer's floor. "Do you still have that knife, Henry?"

"Yeah." his friend replies digging inside his pocket, "I got it right here."

Henry hands him the knife, and he slits the bag.

"Let's see if my thoughts are right about this." the detective utters.

Greg wets the top of his index finger with his tongue, and sticks it inside the plastic. He lifts his hand back up with the white residue on it. The man licks the powder from his finger and pauses to identify the taste. "It's definitely heroin." he says to his friend.

The detective stands folding the knife and gives it back to Henry. "Let's see what else is in these crates." he suggests and returns to get the crow bar.

When Greg comes back with it, he opens the last two wooden boxes at the doorway. He drops the bar out on the ground and looks inside the first one. "Here's some loaded rifle magazines and grenades." he informs his friend.

Gradually, the detective pulls out some of the contents from the second crate.

Both of them gaze a moment, wordless.

Greg lays two of the weapons on the trailer floor, and his friend picks one up.

Henry looks at the detective with a grin on his face. "You and I both know what this is." he mentions observing it, "This is an M-16 with an M203 Grenade Launcher attached to it, brand- spankin'- new."

Greg watches his friend work with the weapon. "I bet there's a lot more in here." he says.

"We'll find out." Henry tells him, "I'll get up there and help ya'. I got another crow bar over there by the back door."

His friend retrieves the tool and climbs in the van with him.

The detective looks at him. "Do you have anything I can carry a few of these in?" he inquires, "I've got another idea."

"Yeah." his friend answers, "I got a few of them ole' burlap sacks over there. They'll hold these weapons."

"Perfect." Greg agrees as Henry watches him grab a weapon out of the pile, "An M72A2 Law Rocket. - I think I'll keep this one of these for later. I might need it."

"I know I would." Henry comments, "Let's see what's in the rest of these crates."

"Good idea." the detective agrees.

Suddenly, their attention is drawn to a vehicle coming down the dirt trail.

Greg and his friend glance at each other.

Swiftly, the detective slings the rocket launcher across his body. He draws his revolver as his friend grabs a magazine for the weapon he has.

Immediately, both of them rush to the rear of the trailer. They sit down on the back edge, and climb down to the ground.

As Greg moves toward the front entrance with his weapon aimed, the vehicle stops. The man takes a glimpse back over his shoulder and sees Henry following with the M-16 rifle.

Abruptly, they hear two doors slam almost simultaneously. The detective reaches the entrance and peeks between the doors.

Dusk has settled in, so visibility is greatly minimized.

The detective sees the officers have passed, and hears them walking on the left side of the barn. He points to the rear and heads toward the back doors.

"Psst." he hears his friend whisper.

Henry catches up with him and hands him the rifle. "Take this." he says, "I'll step out and talk to 'em."

Greg holsters his side arm and takes the M-16. "Be careful." he suggests in a low voice, "I got your back."

His friend nods and heads to the rear entrance.

The detective trails him and takes a position at the doorway.

Henry gives him a glimpse and steps outside. "Can I help you guys with somethin'?" his friend asks when the two officers reach the back of the barn.

"I'm sorry to bother you this late in the evening, sir." one of the policemen says, "Are you Henry Scroggins?"

"That's me." his friend answers.

"I'm Corporal Parks." the man introduces himself, "And this is my partner, Officer Greene. Do you know Detective Greg Hardison?"

"He used to be on the police force about three years ago." Henry replies, "He's a truck driver now, and is probably on the road."

"I guess you haven't heard." the guy mentions, "He was reinstated this morning. We were given your name as a possible friend. My partner and I are trying to determine his whereabouts. Has he been around here?"

"No." Henry answers, "But when I see him, I'll let him know."

"Thanks." the corporal responds.

"Can I ask why you're lookin' for him?" Henry inquires.

"He had a little trouble at his place this morning." the man explains, "We're just making sure he's alright, and we need to ask him a few questions."

"Oh." Henry pauses, "I see. - Did Captain Harris send ya'?"

"No." the officer tells him, "Our lieutenant did. He's concerned about the guy."

"Okay." Henry states, "I'll let Greg know if I see him."

"Thanks for your cooperation." the corporal says.

"You're welcome." Henry responds.

A few seconds later, Greg's friend returns inside the barn. "You heard that, didn't ya'?" he inquires.

"Yeah." the detective says giving him the rifle, "The lieutenant is Moran's eyes and ears in the precinct. – The commissioner is too."

"I think Thompson has something else in mind for you, my friend." Henry believes, "Get outta' here and get the captain. He's been waitin' years to bust Moran. I think this is the break Richard needs."

"Right." Greg agrees, "Let me get these bags together."

"Okay." his friend utters, "Your SKS and bag are by the back door. I'm going out front and piddle around. I wanna' make sure they leave."

Chapter Sixteen

Greg's borrowed Henry's pick up again to carry out his plan.

In the light of the full moon, the man glances back over his shoulder at the two large burlap sacks in the bed. He sees they're still intact and returns his focus to the roadway before him.

The detective's approaching the street leading to the Highway 51 Food Mart.

Suddenly, the guy's phone rings. He presses his earpiece button and answers the call.

"I'm sorry if I'm disturbing you." his wife apologizes, "But I just wanted to hear your voice. We're so worried about you."

"Forgive me for not staying in touch, honey." he responds making his right turn at the intersection, "There's a lot going on right now, - and I'm just trying hard to keep up. Is everybody alright?"

"Yes." she replies, "How are you doing?"

"I'm fine." Greg says, "I'm going to meet with Captain Harris. I was investigating some stolen merchandise."

"Be careful out there, sweetheart." Janna mentions, "I want you back with us soon."

"I will." the detective assures her, "I'll contact you later when things cool down some."

"Okay" his wife agrees, "I love you."

"I love you too." he voices calmly, "Tell Landon the same - and give him a hug for me."

They exchange goodbyes, and Greg ends the call. He gazes ahead a moment in thought, hoping his present plan will rescue the captain.

Shortly, the detective reaches Highway 51 and stops. He sees the coast is clear, so the guy makes a left turn heading back to the city area.

While driving, Greg looks a second time at the burlap sacks through the rear window. "I've got to make this work." he mumbles and faces the roadway in front again.

Suddenly, Greg sees a black car coming towards him in the moonlight's gleam.

The vehicle's coming fast, so he remains calm and alert as it approaches. With ease, the detective pulls his gun from the holster and lays it on the passenger seat. He moves on normally staring the vehicle with patience.

Quickly, the Lincoln Sedan passes and Greg glances at it in his rear view mirror. He sees the car moving on down the roadway with its tinted windows, unsure if it's Moran's men. Apparently, the detective sees the guys didn't notice him if they are. So Greg pulls out his phone. He dials the number to the police station with a thumb and sends it through. The man lays the phone on his lap and listens through his headpiece. Just as he returns his weapon to its holster, someone comes on the line.

"Redwood Springs Police Department?" the detective hears.

"Who is this?" he asks, not recognizing the voice.

"This is Detective Allison." she says, "Who are you?"

"Kim!" the detective exclaims gladly, you're sounding a little hoarse, "It's me! Greg!"

"Oh my god!" Kim responds, astounded, "How have you been, ole' friend? Tara told me you're back!"

"You weren't there when I came in this morning." he tells her, "Chief hired me again."

"That's great!" she voices with joy, "I'm on the evening shift now - but it's nice to have you back."

"Right now, I'm out here trying to get our captain back." Greg mentions.

"Hold on." she asks quietly, "Let me take this call into Captain Harris's office. I've gotta' lot to tell ya'."

"Okay." Greg says and waits for her to return to the line.

Nearly a moment went by, and Kim returns to the phone.

"Hey." she whispers.

"I'm here." he replies, "What's going on?"

"The lieutenant just released Weaver and Beck." Kim informs him, "I also found out he called internal affairs about you. He accused *you* for kidnapping his witness."

"Like hell I did!" Greg replies with rage, "That son -of -a -bitch abducted her and tried to hand-deliver her to Moran! We were trying to stop him!"

"We know that." she responds, "The district attorney has gotten a written testimony from Tia about Cole's murder. Wilkins said he already talked to you. Now he needs *your* report, and that other girl who saw it."

"Kera." he says, "I took her home. There's some officers over there guarding the home now."

"I'll get one of the guy's to get her statement." the lady offers.

"Thanks." the man says.

"No problem." Kim adds, "You know? - I hear that Douglas Moran is bad news. One of my F. B. I. friends says he's been under investigation for the past few years with them. Their informants are giving them leads, but they can't tie the guy to his crimes or the illegal shipments."

"I can." Greg confesses, "I've *got* one of them."

"Are you serious!" she exclaims, astonished, "How in the hell did you pull that off!"

"He was trying to ship it in a rig." he explains, "And I ripped it off to bargain for Captain Harris."

"Damn!" Detective Allison exclaims, "I know you pissed him off bad. He's probably got all of his men looking for you. You're *definitely* gonna' need some help."

"He doesn't know it's me." Detective Hardison explains, "He thinks I'm Albert Jackson, a fake convict who just released from the pen. The guy's convinced that Richard busted me for drugs and I've got an old score to settle with him, one-hundred thousand dollars. – Now, keep that between us. Wilkins knows I've got some merchandise that belongs to Moran. I didn't tell him anything else. He gave me twenty-four hours to get back with him."

"My god!" Kim blurts, "What's in it?"

"Heroine and weapons." Greg states, "Worth twenty million dollars."

"Unbelievable!" she responds, impressed, "The DA.'s gonna' love you. Let's see his lawyers get him outta' that."

"It won't be enough evidence." the man mentions, "He'll deny it, and we won't be able to pin the shipment on him. It's his word against mine. He has to claim the merchandise. – And I'll make him do that."

"How?" Kim wonders.

"You leave that to me," the guy advises her, "but I'll need some help."

"Okay." the lady decides, "Just tell me when and where?"

"Sergeant Maddox was gonna' help me." Greg says, "I really need someone who's more combat-trained."

"Patricia's at lunch right now." Kim informs him, "I can get one of the other guys to fill in until she gets back. Just tell me what you need, and I'll make it happen."

"Alright." he accepts, "Here's the plan."

Chapter Seventeen

About twenty minutes later, Greg approaches Vantage Street on the right. He brakes gently and makes a smooth turn on the roadway. The man creeps down about fifty feet, and pulls into a clear spot by the woods.

He conceals the truck from passing vehicles and shifts to park.

Afterwards, the detective gets out and shuts the door. He dashes to the truck's bed and removes the straps from the bags. The man uses the glow of the full moon to recheck the contents.

Hastening, Greg snatches the sack with the twenty bags of heroine. He scurries to a nearby tree and hides it behind the base. The guy does the same with the sack of seven rifles.

Immediately, the detective returns to the pickup. He hops in the vehicle and slams the door. The man shifts to reverse and backs out of the woods. He straightens the vehicle on the roadway and races back to the intersection.

At the crossing, Greg carefully scans his surroundings. He sees the coast is clear and proceeds across the highway. Briefly, the detective stops. He snatches his cell phone out and calls the precinct again.

"Redwood Springs Police Department, may I help you?" he hears.

"Hi, Patricia." the man greets her, "Can I speak to Kim?"

"Sure." the sergeant says, "She's right here."

Detective Allison comes on the line. "Are you in position?" she asks.

"In about three minutes." he replies.

"I'm on my way." the lady informs him, "The manager already knows about it. She's a friend. I'll call her again en-route."

"Thanks." Greg tells her.

"You bet." Kim responds and he disconnects.

The detective pouches the phone and cruises on past the restaurant bordering the strip mall. He passes through the parking lot and turns right before the stores. The guy drives on to the hotel just feet from the shopping outlets.

Gradually, Greg pulls in a guest- area spot. He parks facing the food franchise. The man glances at the cars resting on each side of him and moves his eyes ahead. The detective has a good view of the restaurant and also the lot surrounding it. So he shifts the vehicle to park and shuts off the engine.

Greg pulls Ned's cell phone out again. He scroll to Moran's number and calls it. The ring sounds one time and the mob boss answers.

"Where are you!" the man asks rudely.

"Here's what I need you to do!" Greg voices bluntly, "Go to Burger Bar at the corner of U. S. 51 and Vantage! Take the captain in there to the back booth! Sit him down away from the window and leave him! When you get outside, I'll tell you where to find your goods close by! I've got three of my buddies scoping that area with rifles! No tricks! If you make a mistake, you'll get shot! And I'll dump this crap all over the city and make money off it! I need some income anyway! One of my friends will tell me when you're done! I'll call you! – Don't screw up!"

Greg disconnects the line and returns the phone to his jacket pocket. He gives a glimpse aside to his rifle then returns his eyes to the franchise before him. The guy rests his elbow upon the door. He gets more comfortable with his sitting position and waits patiently staring the building.

Within a few minutes, the guy spots Detective Allison's yellow Mustang. She's pulling into the little mall on his right, cruising in front of the stores.

The guy observes the vehicle moving to the back area of Burger Bar. "I knew I could count on you, Kim." he mumbles to himself.

Shortly, the man's phone rings. He answers it instantly.

"You should have my new number on your caller I. D." she states, "I got yours from dispatch. Ring me twice, and I'll move in."

"Got ya'." Greg assures her, "I'll come after you in two minutes if you're not out."

" Okay." Kim agrees and he ends the call.

Slowly, the man shifts his view to the intersection. He takes a glimpse at his watch seeing it's almost eight o'clock at night. "After we get Richard?" the detective utters to himself, "This is gonna' get *very* interesting."

Chapter Eighteen

At eight -fifteen, Greg sees a black Lincoln sedan pulling into Burger Bar's parking lot. Another car just like it follows closely behind. The vehicles stop almost simultaneously, blocking at least six of the empty parking spots.

Gradually, he sees the driver of the first getting out wearing a gray suit. The man stands briefly, looking at the restaurant. He scans the surrounding and proceeds to the rear car door. The guy opens it and speaks to someone inside the vehicle.

Next, a dark-suited man emerges from the passenger door of the second sedan.

"Terrance." Greg says to himself, recognizing him from the warehouse.

The detective watches him approach the opened door as the gray-suited guard backs away.

Shortly, Terrance waves for someone to come out. He steps aside and Captain Harris gets out of the vehicle. Mysteriously, the guys stand as Moran's lieutenant talks on his cell phone.

Greg observes as the other men exit the sedans and join them. The group converses a moment, and one of the guards steps away escorting the captain. The two are heading towards the entrance to the restaurant.

The detective rolls down the driver window. He retrieves his phone and holds it down in his hand. The man keeps his eyes on the pair until they enter the franchise.

Quickly, Greg pulls up Kim's number on his phone. He calls it and allows the line to ring twice. The guy disconnects immediately and returns the item to his pouch.

The man shifts his focus to the rear of building. He spots Detective Allison exiting the Mustang with her dark pants suit on. She draws her sidearm and tactically moves toward the back door.

Swiftly, Greg reaches aside for his rifle. He snatches it and flips the lever off the safe position. The man slaps the bottom of the thirty- round magazine and checks the time on his watch.

When Detective Hardison looks up again, he sees Kim going inside the back door. In haste, the guy turns his view to the front of the franchise. He spots Terrance lecturing the group by the sedans.

Greg gets out of the truck and aims his rifle at them. He rests his elbows on the base of his opened window, locking his position to fire comfortably.

The man waits a few seconds, and spots Kim racing out the back door.

She's got the captain by the hand, scurrying back to her car.

The detective moves his eyes back to Moran's guys, seeing they're still unaware that something has happened.

Just as her Mustang passes him, he sees one of the guards rushing out of the restaurant.

The crew member has a palm on the back of his head, holding his handgun with the other.

Quickly, Greg returns inside the truck. He props his weapon on the passenger side and snatches Ned's phone out of his pocket. The detective calls Moran again and closes the truck door.

After one ring, Douglas answers.

The detective ignores his rude greeting and bluntly speaks, "Have your men to approach the intersection where the restaurant is! Go down

Vantage Street about fifty feet! Turn left into the clear area! Look behind the tree in front of you! Call me back when get the merchandise!"

Greg hangs up and rests the phone on the passenger seat with his bag. He watches Terrance and his crew searching around the franchise with handguns, startling customers.

Suddenly, Moran's lieutenant halts and pulls out his cell phone.

The detective observes the brief call and watches him return the phone to his pocket.

Immediately, Terrance points to the sedans while yelling something to his crew. He runs with them to their vehicles.

Suddenly, Greg's distracted by a woman standing near them in the front parking lot. She's holding a mobile phone to her ear, pointing at the guys rushing away.

"That lady's calling the police." he mumbles to himself.

The guy waits for the crew to pull away and moves out of his parking spot. He drives around the rear of the hotel.

The man gets to the opposite side and goes up far enough to see the intersection. He shifts the truck in park and sits. "Well?" he breathes out a long sigh, "I can take the trailer and drop it off somewhere, and hope he doesn't find out who I am, - or I can keep it and try to bust his ass once and for all. - Either way, the bastard will try to kill me." Greg pauses and snickers with a grin. "I think I'll use it as bait." he decides, "The big fish will come for it sooner or later."

Mysteriously, the guy looks left and notices blue flashing lights coming down Highway 51. It's followed by several sets after he spots the first cruiser approaching. The detective hurries retrieving his phone and dials the police station. He listens to a couple of rings and someone answers. "Patricia?" Greg says quickly recognizing her voice, "Call off the squad cars to Burger Bar." the man requests, "They're almost here. I've got this situation under control."

"I'll get right on it." she says.

"Thanks." the detective responds.

As Greg ends the conversation, Ned's phone rings. So he stuffs *his* back in the case and answers the incoming call.

"Is this some damn trick!" Moran exclaims, enraged, "You son -of -a -bitch!"

"You set me up!" Greg yells, "The cops were chasing my girl and she had to put Harris out! Cops are all around him because you put him in the spotlight! So I'm left with nothing! Guess who's paying the bill, hotshot! If you want this trailer back, it's gonna' cost you one million dollars!"

"Damn you!" the mob boss shouts loudly.

Strangely, it sounds like Douglas's phone dropped to the floor. The detective stays silent, listening to glass shattering on the line.

That racket is followed by the sound of items like small furniture being viciously tossed around the room.

While waiting, Greg observes the police cars approaching. They're turning off their bar lights and reducing their speed. Shortly, the vehicles scatter and move in opposite directions.

As the guy stares at one driving away, Douglas returns on the line. Calmly, the detective allows the mob boss to shout with his profanity.

The guy calls him several vulgar names.

The detective pauses for a break in the obscenities, and finally gets his chance to speak. "It's clear you don't want the damn deal!" Greg lashes back, "I'll just take what's mine and dump the rest in the river!" The detective hangs up and sits in his seat patiently.

A few seconds later, the mob boss calls back. "Alright, you bastard!" he yells, "When do we meet!"

"I'll let you know when and where!" Greg informs him, "Just stay by the phone! You bring the money! The trailer will be there! If anybody else shows up, the deal is off!"

The detective disconnects the line. He snickers stuffing the phone back inside his jacket pocket. "You low-down bastard." he mumbles.

Gradually, the man shifts the truck in drive. He pulls out of the parking lot and turns left on Highway 51. The guy accelerates through the changing traffic light and heads on to the precinct.

Chapter Nineteen

A few minutes later, Detective Hardison arrives at the police station. He passes in front of the building and drives on to the employee lot. The man pulls into the parking area, and begins looking for his car. He proceeds down the first aisle towards the fence and spots it. "There she is." the guy whispers in a breath while staring his black Monte Carlo.

Greg pulls beside his vehicle and stops. He leaves the engine running and puts the truck in park. The guy gets out and retrieves his car keys from his pants pocket. He opens the trunk to the car and walks around to the passenger's side of the truck. The detective opens the door and pulls out his rifle. He slings it and does the same with the rocket launcher.

Mysteriously, the man spots a scene across the street. Greg observes closely while reaching for his bag. He lifts its strap over the same shoulder, gazing at the coffee house parking lot. The guy's watching a slender woman in a light-colored dress backing away from something.

Gently, he shuts the passenger door.

As the detective puts his items in the trunk of his car, she dashes towards the street. The man closes the compartment and jogs in her direction drawing his revolver.

The female runs into the roadway and almost gets hit by a minivan. Still, she keeps going. The woman passes through the row of hedges bordering the station's front lot.

Instantly, Greg returns his focus to the coffee house parking area. He notices another slim lady wearing a solid-white pants suit. The bright overhead illumination reveals every feature about her.

Cautiously, the guy reduces to a walk while crossing the street. He locks his eyes upon her as she stands just feet before a white Mercedes.

Gradually, the detective diminishes to a halt just steps in front of her. He can see she's of Indian descent with her long dark hair.

The woman's beautiful with golden- brown skin and a tiny mole on her left cheek.

Gently, Greg points behind to the precinct. "What was that lady running from?" he asks, curious.

The female shrugs her shoulders. "Probably her worst fear." she answers and steps away.

Greg watches the lady walk away in her tight suit, wearing her spandex pants. He notices two budges in the lower back of the lady's jacket, appearing to be the imprints of handguns. "Why are you after her?" he asks in a louder tone, as she faces him in her tucked white blouse.

Slowly, the woman opens the driver door to the Mercedes. "The business between us is personal." the woman responds, "That tramp and my husband have something I want."

"What is it?" Greg inquires holstering his weapon.

"My child." she answers.

The lady gets inside the vehicle and slams the door. She starts the car and swerves around him rolling her eyes. The woman steers right on the roadway and fish tails racing away.

The detective faces the station and lightly shakes his head a couple of times. He sees three uniformed officers coming across the street to meet him.

They're followed by Captain Harris and his brother.

One of the policemen pats him on the shoulder. "Are you alright man?" he asks.

"Yeah." the detective replies, "It's been a very long day."

Richard shakes his hand with a warm smile. "I knew I could count on you." he says, "Kim told me what you've done. That took a lot of guts. – Thanks man."

The captain releases his grip and steps aside.

Wade gives him a handshake and a shoulder tap. "I knew you'd show up here sooner or later." he says, "I'm glad you're on the force again, bro'."

"Me too." Greg admits.

"I recognize that lady who ran in the building." his brother states, "There's something I need to tell ya' before you talk to her."

"I think I will." the detective decides, "She's got something to worry about."

Greg looks at Captain Harris. "Are you okay sir?" he asks.

Richard pats him on the shoulder. "I got roughed up a little bit." he confesses, "But I'll be okay. The men blindfolded me going there and coming back. So I have no clue where the bastard is, or where he lives. I've got a S. W. A. T. team on standby. We have to find Moran and his compound."

"I'll have his whereabouts in the next few hours." Greg informs him, "We've got a lot to talk about. Where's the lieutenant?"

"I've already taken care of it." Richard informs him, "I gave the mayor a call on the way here. He knows all about it. The man's got a warrant out for Thompson's arrest right now. We've got an A. P. B. out on him. But he hasn't been found yet."

"The guy's probably with Moran," Greg responds, "his second boss. – The lieutenant was here. Kim told me he had Weaver and Beck released.

So he must've got the hell outta' here after that. - I've gotta' meet with Douglas later. I'll need heavy backup."

Captain Harris holds up an index finger. "The bastard's got another hostage in the basement - a teenage girl. We've got to find the house to get her." he mentions and pauses a second, thinking. "Also, I heard a young boy's voice upstairs." he remembers, "The girl told me he's Moran's son. Let's go inside and do some planning." the captain tells him and heads toward the building.

"Give me a few minutes." Greg requests, "I have to lock Henry's truck and visit the men's room."

Wade gives him a fist bump. "I'll see you inside bro." he says.

Greg nods and steps away heading back to Henry's truck.

The detective gets to the vehicle and shuts off the engine. He locks the doors and stuffs the key inside his pocket. While returning to the entrance, the man glances right and spots the white Mercedes again.

The lady's parallel parking almost a hundred feet from the coffee house.

Still, the man moves on being driven by his restroom urge.

Quickly, Greg rushes through the double doors. He goes directly for the men's room just feet from the entrance.

Within minutes, the detective walks to the sink area inside. He turns on the faucet and takes a look at himself in the mirror. Briefly, the guy pauses with a short gaze in silence. He brushes across his forehead with the back of a hand, releasing a sigh of relief. The detective holds his head down while washing his hands, listening to someone enter from outside.

Suddenly, Ned's phone rings.

Greg rubs down his jacket quickly to dry the hands. The guy pulls the mobile device from the pocket and checks the caller I. D. "Rivera?" he reads to himself, "I figured I'd hear from you sooner or later."

In a hurry, the detective converts to a southern accent when he answers. "This is the Roadside Truck Stop." he says, "Can I help ya'?"

"Who is this?" Rivera asks bluntly.

"Ned left this phone on the counter when he went to pump fuel." Greg tells him, "You want me to have him to call ya'?"

"Yes." the boss hesitates, "Where are you located?"

"We're in the dip here in Jaw-ja." the detective replies, "We sittin' in a town called Wildwood, not far from Chattanooga. You ought ta' come visit us sometime. We'd be much obliged."

"Just have Ned to call me A.S.A.P." Rivera requests.

"Asap?" Greg blurts out, "My name ain't Asap. I'm Ben."

"Damnit!" the boss gets frustrated, "Have him to contact me immediately!"

Rivera hangs up.

Gently, the detective stuffs the phone back inside his pocket. The man hears someone giggling. So he turns around and notices a fellow officer approaching a sink in uniform.

The guy smiles with a light shake of the head. "We missed that humor around here." he comments, "Ned's over there sittin' in the lieutenant's office. He came in just after Thompson left."

Greg paces towards the door and looks back over his shoulder. "Why did the trucker want to see him?" he inquires.

"To get his tractor and trailer." the coworker responds, "He filed a report for theft earlier."

"We'll find it." the detective mentions, opening the door with a grin.

Greg steps out of the restroom and instantly locks his eyes on the woman who'd run across the street.

She's sitting quietly on the sofa by the water fountain. The lady appears nervous, staring the entrance behind him. The guy takes a glance back over his shoulder, following her eyes. He sees no one coming in. So the man continues on his route.

Suddenly, the detective's distracted by the captain emerging from the lieutenant's office.

Richard gives him a glimpse and tilts his head for him to join him. He has a puzzled look upon his face as Greg strolls to meet him. Captain Harris folds his arms and stands staring inside the room.

The detective gets there and sees Ned sitting comfortably in the lieutenant's chair.

"What are you doing here?" he inquires recognizing the old truck driver in his red cap.

"I'm waitin' for Lieutenant Thompson." the man answers, standing.

Captain Harris rushes to the desk, and Ned moves away in haste. Richard snatches open the center drawer and pulls out a brown envelope. He holds it up facing Greg. "The lieutenant forgot to take his deposit with him." Richard says, "One of our officers heard him talking about it on the phone."

"You wanna' use the funds as evidence?" the detective suggests, stepping inside.

"Everything we can get." the captain responds.

"Somebody stole my rig." Ned blurts out, "I filed a report. - They can have the damn trailer. I just want my truck back."

Greg and Richard look at each other. The detective holds out a palm towards Ned.

"May I?" he asks the captain.

Richard returns his eyes to the elderly driver. "Be my guest." he approves, "I think this trucker has a need to know."

Greg moves closer to the desk and stands. "I have some questions for you, Ned." he interrogates, "Are you the rightful owner of a red freightliner, truck number 998441?"

"Yes I am." the driver confesses.

"Carrying trailer number 652371?" the detective adds.

"That's right." the guy admits.

"You're under arrest for attempting to smuggle heroin and weapons for resale." Greg informs him, and begins stating his Miranda Rights.

"Wait a minute!" the man demands, terrified, "It's not mine! My truck was stolen! They must've loaded that on the trailer when it was taken!"

"If you lie to me again, I'll put you in jail myself." Greg threatens him, "We have the suspect in custody. He stole the truck from an old airfield off Highway 51. How did it get there, Ned?"

The trucker stutters trying to answer, worrisome. "I drove it there!" he admits, "But that ain't my merchandise!"

"Still, you're an accessory." the detective tells him, "You're facing from ten to twenty years for your part in the crime."

"Please Mr. Officer." Ned begs with a calm tone, "I just wanna" get back home to my family. Can we work somethin' out?"

Greg folds his arms gently with a sigh. "We've impounded the tractor and trailer as evidence." he mentions, "We'll also need the phone that was found on the seat."

"You can have it!" the man offers, desperate, "Everything!"

"Go wait in the captain's office." the detective orders, "He'll get a safe place for you to stay tonight. You can pick up your truck and phone here in the morning."

"Thank you, sir." the driver says, appreciatively.

"Don't breathe a word of this to anyone." Greg warns him, "If you do, I'll revoke the deal."

"I won't." Ned assures him, "You have my word."

The old gentleman passes him and moves on to the door. "Where's the office?" the trucker asks.

"Go across the main floor and it's down the hall." Richard informs him, "The first one on the left."

When Ned moves on to the office, Captain Harris stares Greg with a smile.

"Well?' Richard utters, "You've taken care of that. How do we handle the shipment?"

"I'll need backup." the detective replies, "I need Wade to get the F. B. I. in on this too."

"I already have." they hear, and both of them face the doorway.

Greg's brother steps inside the office. "We have a team that's completed an assignment in Princeton, about fifteen miles from here." the agent explains, "I've briefed the director about these incidents. When I mentioned Moran, he didn't hesitate granting me permission to use them. What's the plan?"

Chapter Twenty

Detective Hardison has finished explaining his plan to Wade and Richard. He's preparing to leave after discussing some other private matters with the captain. The man heads for the entrance then turns back to see his brother again.

As the guy walks to the desk where Wade's seated, he looks at the woman in the flowered dress again. He observes a female officer trying to talk to her and see she's still jittery.

Finally, Greg turns his eyes away and strolls on. He approaches his brother on the computer researching something. The man places a hand upon Wade's shoulder. "I'm going to check on my wife and son." he says, "I'll call ya' after I leave the house."

"Okay." the agent responds, "You need me to go with ya'?"

"No." the detective answers, "I'll be alright."

"Call if you need me." his brother tells him.

"I will." Greg assures him, "What are you looking for?"

Just then, a picture of the woman in the flowered dress appears on the computer screen.

Wade snickers. "Dr. Tamela Perkins." he utters, "She's a psychiatrist on the other side of the city. The lady's from Tampa, Florida, where she practiced her profession for ten years. Tamela was busted for tax evasion nearly a year ago. Douglas Moran paid her bail money. The doctor was defended by his attorneys, and now she's here. I wonder why?"

"Interesting." the detective mumbles, curious. "Is she his girlfriend?"

"I think so." the agent agrees, "Probably his mistress. - Check this out, bro."

His brother goes to a different screen with another female's photo. "This is one of the cold cases we had a few months ago." Wade adds, "The mob boss was cleared of all charges for his wife's murder. The authorities didn't have enough evidence to prosecute him. The reports stated that Moran shot her and tossed her overboard in the Florida Keys. No body was found. Her name is Eleanor Moran. She was into smuggling precious stones and jewels. The lady was a multi-millionaire with a sinister organization as well. Actually, the woman pulled Douglas from the streets and made him. Eleanor was known for carrying two fancy nine- millimeter handguns. She had two federal arrests. No convictions."

"I'll be damned." Greg whispers staring the picture, "That's her."

"What are you talking about?" Wade turns to him, puzzled.

"That's the lady I saw in the coffee house parking lot." the detective remembers.

"It can't be." the agent says, giving him a confused look, "The lady's deceased."

"Like hell she is." Greg responds and heads for the entrance.

Detective Hardison rushes out the door and looks down the street. The guy spots the Mercedes resting under the streetlamp as before. So he goes down the steps and begins walking towards it. He veers his eyes back over his shoulder, and sees his brother following closely.

Suddenly, the vehicle's headlights turn on. The engine roars, and it spins out making a U-turn.

The car fishtails swiftly and races down the highway. The agent catches up with Greg as he stands in the middle of the road.

"If you're right, -" Wade pauses taking a deep breath, "we've got *two* big problems."

"Three." the detective adds, "Rivera's probably coming here too, and I don't believe he'll be alone."

"I'll bet Eleanor's not by herself either." Wade comments, "When you see that lady, her posse is close by. The woman's dangerous. She doesn't have any warrants out on her. But the lady could be using her maiden name so she can't be tracked. Her son has the same last name."

"What is it?" he asks his brother.

"Eleanor Leyton." the agent informs him, "The son's name is Adrian Leyton. If you saw her, she could be looking for him. Douglas might have the boy with him."

"She mentioned the word *child* when I was talking to her in parking lot." Greg remembers, "I believe you're right."

Greg steps back to the sidewalk with his brother walking beside him. "I'm going to my stepmother's house to see Janna and Landon." he decides.

"If I don't hear from you in an hour, I'll be over there." the agent assures him.

"Alright." the detective agrees and gives his brother a fist bump, "I'll talk to you soon."

Chapter Twenty-One

Just minutes after Greg's departure, Ned's cell phone rings again. He checks the caller I. D., and sees it's Rivera calling back. The detective answers. "Are you the guy that called here before?" he says with a southern accent.

"What are you still doing with Ned's phone?" the boss inquires harshly.

"He used a card at the pump." Greg informs him, "The driver finished and left without coming back in. We tried to set him up in here, but our registers are messed up."

"That idiot!" Rivera blurts out, enraged.

"Ned came in the store to get some snacks." the detective mentions, "I forgot to tell ya' before. The trucker said he's going back to Redwood Springs. They forgot to put some things on his load."

"Damnit!" the boss shouts, "That son -of -a -bitch!"

Rivera disconnects the line.

Slowly, Greg returns the phone to his pocket. "Well?" he mumbles, "I think the bastard's coming here."

Suddenly, *his* phone rings. He reaches for the pouch and struggles a bit pulling it out. The guy sees his wife's name on the display and hurries answering the call.

"Honey?" his wife whispers in a nervy voice, "There's a man here looking for you."

"Are you okay?" the detective asks, instantly worried.

"We're in the attic." she says softly, "Gary and Daddy's down there with him. The rest of us are up here."

"Stay where you are!" he orders her, "I'll be there in five minutes!"

Greg steps on the gas and storms down Eighth Avenue. He tucks the phone back in the case and starts passing every vehicle in front of him.

Shortly, the man approaches Felton Drive. He steers on the street and spins the tires racing on.

Mysteriously, the detective notices a gray Crown Victoria under the streetlight ahead. The car's parked in front of the two police cruisers guarding the house. The guy begins slowing down rapidly.

Swiftly, Greg steers to the small wood line before the home. He goes to the closest part and stops. The detective shoves the gear lever in park and shuts the engine off. He opens the trunk with the remote.

Hastening, the man emerges from the car. He dashes to the rear of the vehicle and yanks his rifle from the compartment. The guy closes the trunk gently and hurries toward the house.

Silently, Greg moves in closer with a tactical aim. He glances aside and sees one of the guard's bodies lying upon the lawn. The man takes a glimpse at the gun wounds to the abdomen. He sees the officer is still breathing, but unconscious.

The detective proceeds on to the front door. He gets there and positions on the side near the knob. Just as Greg points the barrel of his weapon up, he hears a gunshot inside.

When Gary yells in pain, the detective slams his shoulder against the door. He charges inside aiming his rifle.

Immediately, the guy sees a uniformed officer standing over his stepbrother with a handgun. The policeman raises the weapon towards him, and the detective fires three rounds into his chest. The officer stumbles back over his stepbrother's feet and falls flat on the floor.

Gary rises to a sitting position, holding the bloody wound in his side. "They're down the hall," he strains to say, "probably in the attic. The other cop is shootin' down there too."

Greg moves on down the hallway stepping lightly. He proceeds silently with his SKS pointing ahead at eye level.

Suddenly, a gunshot sounds from one of the two rooms at the end.

A female's scream fills the air before him, and she's begging for mercy.

He can even hear his son crying hard, forcing him to walk faster.

"Open the damn door!" Greg hears a man yell, "Give me the Yang girl, and I might just spare the rest of you!"

The detective holds the rifle upright and shifts closer to the opened door. He tilts his head forward and peeks at the lieutenant looking up the stairs to the attic.

Swiftly, Greg steps into the doorway and locks his aim at the man. "Dalton!" he yells pointing the barrel at the guy's back.

The lieutenant turns around quickly and raises the handgun towards him.

Greg shoots two rapid shots in Dalton's upper torso, flinging him back to the wall. As the detective creeps closer, he stares the lieutenant's body dropping to a sitting position.

Gradually, Joseph lifts his bowed head and locks eyes with the Greg. He snickers, and spits on the floor between his legs. "You pathetic son -of -a -bitch!" he blurts disrespectfully, "You'll pay for this!"

The detective moves nearer with his weapon aimed at the lieutenant's chest. "You're under arrest for attempted murder, assault, and kidnapping!" he informs him harshly, "You better hope nobody's hurt up there, or *you'll* pay for it! You fake bastard!"

As Greg cites his Miranda Rights to him, Joseph interrupts with a giggle, "You won't get a chance to take me in." he groans.

Swiftly, the lieutenant points the gun at him.

Greg discharges another round into his chest.

Dalton's head bows lifelessly, and he releases the firearm.

Greg looks up at the attic entrance. "Janna!" he shouts, "It's me honey! It's safe! You can come out!"

Quickly, his wife opens the door crying. The detective can see his son's head looking down beside her.

"Is anybody shot?" the guy asks, worrisome.

"No." Janna answers, breathing nervously, "He told us to come out. We were scared once he started shooting the door. So all of us laid down on the floor. He missed us."

Hastening, Greg straps the rifle across his back. He goes up the stairs and lifts Landon into his arms. The man heads back down to the bedroom with his wife following closely behind him.

When they get to the bottom, Janna reaches for Landon. She pulls their son from his arms. "I've got him." his wife says.

Greg goes back up to the attic entrance. He meets Tia looking down at him, holding her child. "Hand him to me." he tells her, and she does so. The man returns to the bottom again and stands the kid on the floor.

After Tia comes down with her mother, the guy climbs the stairs a third time. He reaches for Janna's mother. "Come on, Mrs. Allen." he tells her, grabbing her as she steps down following him, "I've got ya'.'" The man descends to the surface with her cautiously.

After the detective helps everyone to the bedroom floor, he rushes to the living room.

The guy gets there and sees his stepfather trying to comfort Gary. "I'm calling for help Mr. Allen." he decides, looking at his stepbrother's waist wound, "He's losing a lot of blood."

"He needs a hospital." the stepfather agrees.

"And so do you." the detective says looking at his bloody shoulder.

"I'll be fine." Mr. Allen tells him, "I can drive myself down there."

"No, you're not." Greg responds and retrieves his phone.

In haste, the detective dials the police dispatcher. He listens to one ring, and someone answers the line.

"Redwood Springs Police Department." she states, "Sergeant Maddox speaking."

"Patricia?" he says, "This is Detective Hardison. I'm at 2601 Felton Drive. I need EMS sent here immediately. Send five ambulances. I have multiple gunshot victims, two innocent civilians and three officers. The two suspects who did the shooting are down. They were two of our guys, and one of them is the lieutenant. Both are deceased. We'll also need a coroner." Greg heads for the front door, "I'm going to check the status of the officer outside."

While rushing to the front yard, he can hear the sergeant requesting for emergency units and police support on another line. The detective dashes from the home and approaches the policeman's body on the lawn. He kneels down quickly and feels for a pulse. "The officer out here is still alive." he reports, "His chest is rising and he needs help immediately. The victim has two gunshot wounds to the abdomen, and has lost a lot of blood."

"I've dispatched multiple E. M. S. units." Patricia responds, "You have additional backup coming for you, and they should be there in a few minutes. Kim got back from a crime scene about twenty minutes ago. Wade told her you were going to the Allen residence, and she raced out the door heading your way. You should see her any moment. Captain

Harris and your brother left here ten minutes ago to check on you. I'll call and let them know. Are you alright?"

"I'm fine." he admits standing, "Thanks for asking."

"Anything for a friend." she comments, "You be careful."

"I will." Greg tells her watching Detective Allison's car pull in front of the home.

"And one last thing," Patricia adds, "the director of Internal Affairs just left for the night. The guy was hanging around here interrogating everybody. He's got some good news for you."

"What?" the detective inquires, suddenly puzzled.

"I'll let the captain tell you when he gets there." she answers, "You take care and keep in touch."

"I appreciate your help." he mentions kindly, watching Kim approach him.

"No problem." the sergeant tells him and disconnects the call.

Detective Allison gets to him and lightly pats him on the shoulder. "Are you okay?" she inquires and glances at the wounded officer lying on the ground.

"I'm fine." he replies.

"He's the officer who lives across the street." she states, "He lives alone. - Where's the other guard Richard sent here?"

"Inside, -" Greg responds pointing behind him, "deceased. The lieutenant's dead too. He's in the back room."

"Do you mind if I take a look inside?" she asks.

"You're a partner *and* friend." he reminds her, "Be my guest."

He follows her in the house and she greets Janna and the other members in the house. Kim walks slowly staring the deceased officer lying on the living room floor. "He's not Johnson." she mentions, "Somebody switched them. - That's Corporal Parks."

Greg looks at him closer, remembering the name. "The lieutenant sent him and Officer Greene to Henry's place earlier. They were trying to find me there, but he steered them away."

"Can I check out the back room?" Detective Allison requests.

"Sure." Greg agrees, "Go ahead. – And thanks for helping me with the rescue."

"You're welcome." Kim responds with a smile, and proceeds on down the hallway.

Shortly, Detective Hardison's attention is drawn to a hand wrapping around his waist. He turns around to his wife holding their son. "Honey? I'm sorry I got all of you in this mess." he apologizes.

"It's not your fault, baby." she explains, softly resting a hand on his cheek, "They followed you home and threatened our family. All of us understand that. We're with you until this is over."

Janna gives him a light kiss on the lips. "It's gonna' be alright." she assures him.

The detective holds them in his arms. "I know it will." he responds, "I promise."

Chapter Twenty-Two

In almost fifteen minutes, Detective Hardison is out on the porch with his wife and sees a pair of headlights coming up the roadway. They're followed by a second and third pair, all with blue lights flashing on top.

When the first car gets closer, the guy recognizes Captain Harris's vehicle.

Just then, Greg notices bright red lights behind them flashing at the intersection. He rushes back inside the house with his wife trailing closely behind him. The man approaches Gary and kneels beside him. He lays his hand on his stepbrother's shoulder.

"Hang in there, man." the detective tells him, "E.M.S. is almost here."

Lightly, Greg pats Mr. Allen's uninjured arm. "I'll come to the hospital and see both of you." he tells him.

Gary grabs his forearm just as the sound of sirens fills the air. "Don't worry about us." he groans, "You keep focusing on your job. I'm glad you saved our lives. They were probably gonna' kill us. Thanks, man. I think I speak for all of us."

The detective looks at his stepfather nodding with a smile.

"We'll be fine, son." Mr. Allen assures him, "Go ahead and do your job. I know you've got your hands full."

Greg gives them a warm grin and stands slowly. He turns around to his wife behind him and hugs her with his child. The guy lifts Landon into his arms. He wipes the tears from his cheeks gently. "It's gonna' be alright son." he whispers with a smile, "I want you to relax and try to get some sleep, okay?" he says and Landon nods, "It's past your bedtime."

The kid gives him a sad look. "Are you leaving again, Daddy?" he asks.

"Just for a little while?" the detective responds, touching the boy's nose with an index finger, "When you open your eyes in the morning, I'll be right here with you. I promise, okay?"

Landon nods again and wraps his arms around Greg's neck.

Suddenly, their attention is drawn to Captain Harris and Wade greeting them. The emergency personnel follow with equipment and hurries to administer aid to the victims.

As they move out of the way, Janna takes the child back into her arms.

The detective gives both a kiss on the cheek. "I'll see you before I leave." he says to them.

She nods and joins her mother observing the paramedics working.

Greg, Wade, and Richard heads for the entrance as crime scene personnel enter to investigate.

The detective directs the coroner to the dead bodies and faces the captain. "We've got to end this problem tonight," he mentions, "once and for all."

"When you left, total chaos erupted." the captain explains, "Phone calls started coming in like wildfire. Moran's men are hitting almost every bar and night club in the city. They're looking for the shipment. Our units are stretched thin trying to handle those calls. The bastards are harassing the owners and customers to get information. I've got the sheriff department in on this too. Some of their guys should be outside now with ours."

Wade pats Richard on the shoulder. "Like I said, I'll get the F. B. I. team from Princeton to join us." he adds, "If we need more, all I have to do is make a phone call."

The Detective Hardison holds up his index finger and looks at the captain. "You said Moran's got a hostage in the basement, right?"

"Yes." Richard answers, "Her name is Lori Caldwell. She told me. I ran a search on her. She's the daughter of a Florida senator. The teenager's been missing for nearly two days. If you find out where he is, wait for backup before you get her. I don't want you to go in there alone."

Captain Harris places his hand upon Greg's shoulder. "You wanna' go outside and brief the guys about your plan tonight?" he suggests, "Maybe you can give them a little pep talk, lieutenant."

Greg stares him wordless, with a puzzled expression.

Detective Allison joins them after conversing with Tia and her mother. She shakes hands with Richard and Wade, greeting them with a smile.

The captain looks at Greg again. "It's been a busy night in the mayor's office." he continues explaining, "The district attorney and director of internal affairs were in a meeting with him about Dalton. They had Tara in the office with them. She told them everything."

"That's good." Detective Hardison replies.

"There's more." Richard adds, "They opened an investigation on Commissioner Baker for hiring the lieutenant and creating his fake identity. - I've been on the phone with the mayor ever since you left. The guys appointed *me* to be the acting commissioner starting Monday morning. - Your name also came up in the meeting."

"For what?" Greg responds, becoming defensive, "All I've done is steal an illegal shipment from a criminal to save you."

Richard pats him on the shoulder with a grin, "Wilkins's mind is hard as a brick to convince. I don't know how Tara and you done it. But for you, they checked your credentials and decided to promote you to lieutenant."

"I didn't want any recognition for rescuing you, sir." Greg states, "I did that because we're friends."

"I know." the captain says, "But I didn't have anything to do with their decision. You were chosen by *them*. - The mayor sent those extra men outside for *you*."

Richard takes a glimpse at the door and points to the crew outside, "Now get out there." he orders him with a smile, "We've got a job to finish, my friend."

As Captain Harris lowers his arm, Wade and Kim congratulates the new lieutenant with a handshake.

Afterwards, Greg heads for the entrance readjusting the rifle strap across his chest. He steps on the porch with his eyes scanning the rows of police cars outside. They're parked on both sides of the street with five ambulances positioned in the middle.

Hastening, the guy steps aside for the paramedics exiting with gurneys. He looks where the officer was lying who lives across the street. The man sees the policeman has already been transported to an ambulance already.

Tia and her mother pass with the child and tells him "Thank you", while being escorted by two officers to the front yard.

Shortly, Greg's focus is suddenly diverted by a third stretcher passing beside him. As he stares at Dalton's body going by, the feeling of rage takes him over. He continues watching as they transport the deceased man off the porch.

Eventually, the ambulances begin rushing away from the scene with two police escorts.

He observes the C. S. I. team sealing off the area with yellow caution tape.

The city, county, and state officers are moving into the street. They're gathering near a streetlamp across from the Allen residence.

After a glimpse at a few neighbors watching from their porches, Greg goes on down the steps. He crosses the yard to meet the crowd. The new lieutenant approaches one of the sergeants on duty and gets his attention. "Can you have the officers to turn their engines off, please?" he requests, glancing at the name tag, "I need to brief them about tonight's operation."

"Sure thing, sir." the officer responds, and heads away to the other policemen.

Greg waits upon the lawn until the patrolmen assemble under the streetlight again.

Gradually, he paces in the roadway until he notices all eyes are on him. "For the one's who don't know me!" he speaks loudly, "I'm Lieutenant Greg Hardison! First, I'd like to thank you for your support and participation! Our mission tonight, is to stop the mob operations around here, and keep you alive! Nobody flies solo from this point on! You ride with a partner, or travel in pairs with cruisers if you're alone! I want you to check every bar, nightclub, and even on the streets! If you see any of those suited bastards causing trouble, arrest their asses and haul them in! None of those son -of -a -bitches will get out on bond!"

Greg turns back to Richard standing behind him. "Can we arrange that, sir?" he asks him.

"We sure can." the captain agrees retrieving his cell phone, "I'll get right on it."

The lieutenant faces the group again, "When you need backup?" he continues speaking, "Call for it! If need a *bus* to haul those bastards downtown, do it! I want that damn organization *out* of here! Because the *mob* doesn't own this city! The *taxpayers* do, and they pay us to do a job! So let's get on it! And remember!" he reiterates, "Stick together! I really appreciate your help! Thank you!"

Greg looks back to Wade. "Can you do me a favor?" he asks.

"I'm already on it." his brother guesses his request, "Your answer is coming behind you. There are more agents on their way."

The lieutenant returns his focus to the front. While watching the squad cars scatter to their patrols, he observes two vehicles moving towards him. The guy stares them until they pass under a streetlight. "Two federal agents?" he wonders.

"Eight." Wade corrects him, "Four in each car. - I asked these guys to come early because I knew you'd need em'. They're heavily armed. Two of these agents will stay here with a couple of *your* officers. The other men and Detective Allison are coming with me. I've got another unit headed to E.R. for Gary and your stepfather. The captain wants Tia and her family to stay at the station tonight."

"Kim won't disappoint you." the lieutenant tells him, "She's just as tough as Rhonda was, - if not better."

"Richard spoke highly about you and her." his brother mentions, "She's a good cop and a military veteran. I can use her expertise and knowledge out there. I'll take care of her."

"I know you will bro'." the lieutenant responds.

Just as more vehicles pull away, the government cars park in their spots. The occupants emerge leaving their headlights on.

Greg watches them until they approach, all eight of them wearing their black tactical gear. When the men reach him with their dark face coverings pulled up, they begin introducing themselves. The agents also greet Captain Harris and steps away with Wade for a briefing.

Richard stretches his hand out to Greg with a smile. The lieutenant shakes it.

"Congratulations." the captain says, "Now make sure you get your ass back here in one piece."

"I'll give it my best shot, sir." Greg replies and releases the hand.

"I know you will." Richard adds.

"I have to see my wife and son before I go." the lieutenant informs him, stuffing his hand in his pants pocket, "I need a favor from you too."

"Alright." the captain responds, "What is it?"

Greg gives him a key. "Can you get Henry's truck back to him?" he asks, "It's in the employee parking lot."

"Sure." Richard agrees, "I'll get a couple of guys to get it out there. One can trail the other."

The lieutenant steps away, heading back to the house. He lifts up the caution tape and goes under it. As the man walks to the porch, he's met by one of the crime scene investigators in charge.

"I need to ask you some questions, sir." the guy requests and points to the rifle strapped on him. "That's the weapon that was used to kill the two suspects in the house, correct?"

"Yes." Greg replies.

"What kind of rifle is that?" the man inquires, pulling out a notepad and pen to write.

"It's a Norinco SKS semi-automatic rifle." the lieutenant answers.

"We'll talk about the living room first." the investigator decides, "The witnesses stated that Corporal Parks aimed a handgun at you, justifying your defense to fire. Do you agree with their testimony?"

"I sure do." Greg responds.

"Did the same action occur in the bedroom with the second victim?" the guy interrogates more.

"Exactly." the lieutenant agrees, "I'll write a report when I get back to the station."

"That'll be fine." the man tells him, "A determination can be made with the information gathered inside, and my interrogation with you. I declare both incidents to be justifiable homicides. Thanks for your cooperation."

"You're welcomed." the lieutenant utters and steps around him to move on.

Greg goes in the house and sees his wife standing with her mother. So he maneuvers by some investigators and approaches them.

Janna gives him a kiss on the lips and rests her hand upon his shoulder.

He greets Mrs. Allison and gives the lady a hug. "Where's Landon?" he asks, turning his focus back to the wife.

"He's asleep on the sofa." she says.

The lieutenant glances at his son, then looks into his wife's eyes. "I'll get back as soon as I can." he assures her.

"Please be careful out there." she stresses, "God knows I don't want you to get hurt. I can't stop worrying about you."

"Like I said, -" he pauses, gently grasping her waist," I'll be here when you wake up in the morning, and all of this will be over. I promise."

"Okay." she sighs, feeling some relief, "I'll be waiting for you."

"I love you." Greg reminds her with a hug.

"I love you too." Janna responds, and they release.

"Tell Gary I need to use his truck." he mentions.

"You know where the keys are." she informs him.

"I believe so." the lieutenant remembers, "In the ignition?"

"You got it." his wife adds with a smile.

"Keep me informed about his condition, *and* Mr. Allen's." he requests.

"If they get worse, I'll call you." she says.

They exchange goodbyes, and he steps to the sofa. The man gives his son a light kiss on the cheek and heads for the front doorway.

Greg walks out on the porch and goes down the steps. He turns right moving to the paved driveway, and veers his eyes back to the street. The guy notices Wade conversing with Richard at the edge of the lawn.

Coincidentally, his brother looks at him. "Are you ready to take off?" he asks loudly.

The lieutenant nods.

Wade gives him a thumb up, and he returns the same.

Richard gestures with a wave. "We're on standby!" the man assures him, "Be careful!"

Greg mocks the captain's hand motion and heads on around the house. He gets behind the home and follows the wide trail of small rocks from the pavement.

The path curves behind the home and expands to a large graveled parking area. The guy gazes beyond the family vehicles and spots Gary's black truck by the light pole.

As the lieutenant strolls to the day cab tractor, he stares it resting upon the grass. The rig is a newer model International with a glossy finish. The man approaches the vehicle and opens the door. He lifts the rifle and strap over his head, holding it in his left hand. The guy uses the other arm to pull himself up the steps.

Quickly, Lieutenant Hardison climbs into the cab. He slides into the seat and props the weapon upright on the passenger floor. The man leans the barrel against the door, propping it against the seat. Greg turns the key one click and allows the truck to go through its startup cycles.

While the tractor does so, the guy pulls his revolver out of the holster. Again, he makes sure the chamber is fully loaded and returns it to the holder. The lieutenant reaches for the key and starts the engine. He powers on the headlights and waits for the air pressure to build.

Shortly, Greg shuts the door. He releases the brakes and shifts the vehicle in gear. The guy eases off the clutch and begins rolling towards the driveway.

The man moves across the gravel and continues on to the street. He gets to roadway and makes eye contact with Captain Harris. The lieutenant waves a final time as his brother faces the tractor.

In haste, Greg steers left onto the street. He rolls to the side of his car as it rests parallel to the wood line. The guy stops and climbs down from the truck. He goes to his vehicle and opens the driver door. The lieutenant retrieves his keys and depresses the trunk button. He slams the door and rushes to the rear of the car.

Instantly, the man reaches inside the compartment for his bag. He slings it over his shoulder and does the same with the Law Rocket Launcher.

After closing the trunk, Greg remote locks the vehicle with his key ring. He dashes back to the truck and climbs into the cab. The man tosses the items in the passenger seat in a hurry. He prepares the vehicle to drive and pulls away.

Immediately, the lieutenant races up the roadway.

Chapter Twenty-Three

Minutes later, the lieutenant arrives at Highway 51. He makes a left turn and rapidly restores to his normal speed. Suddenly, his phone rings. The man uses his earpiece to answer the call.

"I didn't mean to bother ya', if I did." he hears, recognizing Henry's voice, "I just wanted to make sure you're alright."

"No problem, man." Greg says, "I was hoping you were still awake."

"I was gonna' stay up a few more hours for ya'." Henry responds. "Did ya' run into Thompson?"

"Yeah." the guy replies, "He's dead."

"What happened to him?" his friend wonders.

"I had to shoot him." Greg confesses, "My wife and child were in danger. He came to her parent's house looking for a witness to last night's murder. Janna's brother and stepfather were shot."

"I understand." Henry states, "Tell your wife my heart and prayers are with her family. – From what I've been hearing, Thompson had it comin' someday. He was making a lot of enemies at the station. - They're gonna' need a new lieutenant."

"I *am* the lieutenant." Greg admits.

"Get outta' here!" his buddy exclaims, astounded.

"I'll tell you everything when I get time." the man mentions, "Right now, I have to get that trailer and go. I have to finish my part of the plan. I've got Richard and Wade involved."

"Good." Henry agrees, "I'll have the gate open when ya' get here."

"Thanks." Greg responds and disconnects the call..

The guy checks his mirrors and tries to tuck the phone in the case.

Coincidentally, it rings again.

He lifts the mobile device and glances at the screen. "Tara?" he utters to himself then answers the call.

"I just wanted to touch base with ya'." she explains, "I'm leaving for the night, and I wanted to congratulate you. I heard about your promotion."

"I appreciate it." the guy replies.

"Also." the lady adds, "I thought you'd like to know about the woman from the coffee house. Two of Moran's men came and picked her up in a black Lincoln. The female in the Mercedes gave them a drive- by and shot the windows out. She got away from the officer who was chasing her. He said she drove like a race car driver. We didn't even get a tag number."

"Did anybody get hurt?" Greg asks.

"No." Tara replies, "We checked on them. It happened a few feet from the building. They ducked down before she fired. The woman sped away and left them with shattered windows."

"Her name is Eleanor Moran." the lieutenant informs her, "I saw the woman outside earlier. The lady's appears to be bold and aggressive."

"Douglas's wife?" Tara inquires.

"Yeah." the lieutenant concurs, "She's supposed to be dead. I'll explain it to you when I get time."

"Okay." Ms. Spencer agrees, "You be careful out there."

"Alright." he tells her.

Both exchanged goodnights, and Greg ends the call.

The guy looks ahead and spots the food mart he'd visited earlier. So he starts slowing down before reaching the intersection.

Greg gets closer and notices something suspicious in the store parking lot. "Well, I'll be damned." he mumbles engaging his right turn signal, "There she is."

The man observes Eleanor getting in her white Mercedes at the fuel pump. He also sees six black cars of the same model parked on her left side.

As the lieutenant approaches the crossing, he glances at some of the vehicles turning on their headlights.

The guy brakes gently and steers right on Langston Branch Road, passing the side of the store. He accelerates quickly over the posted speed limit, which is forty-five miles per hour.

The man checks his side mirror and sees Eleanor pulling out on the roadway.

Afterwards, Greg spots the other vehicle pulling out behind her.

The Mercedes faces his direction, glaring its headlamps.

As the vehicle continues coming his way, he can see the remaining cars doing the same. Instantly, Greg floors the gas pedal. He excels to seventy miles per hour. The guy doesn't want to be followed, because it'll put him at risk. Also, he can't allow himself to place Henry in danger either. He checks the scene behind him again and notices their headlights are smaller. So the man maintains his speed, and proceeds on down the left-bending road.

Within minutes, the lieutenant spots the glossy street sign ahead on the left. He remembers the intersection from earlier today, as it rests under the moonlight's glow. The guy looks in the driver mirror again and sees no one following him.

Greg brakes rapidly and steers left onto Deer Creek Road. He straightens the tractor quickly and accelerates to resume his speed. The man knows he has only one curve before arriving at Henry's barn. So the lieutenant's hoping he's far enough ahead, still being nearly five miles away.

The guy checks the rear view again and glances at a distant row of lights. He shifts his eyes to the speedometer, reading seventy-two miles per hour. The lieutenant has the gas pedal floored, traveling the vehicle's top speed. So all he can do is hope they don't speed up and get closer.

Shortly, Greg can see the huge curve ahead about three hundred feet away. It's shallow, and he knows the road straightens in front of Henry's property. The man takes one more glimpse at the vehicles trailing him, assuring the distance is the same.

In a hurry, the guy surges into the curve. He steers slightly to the left, hugging the yellow line. The lieutenant disappears from view with the bordering wood line.

Hastening, Greg turns off his lights. He uses the moon's illumination to see the partly shadowed roadway. Just as the pavement straightens, the guy spots a white fence on his right. He can see the opening where the lamp post is lit.

Immediately, the lieutenant brakes hard without skidding. He turns into the gate and notices Henry opening the barn door. Quickly, Greg rolls down the driver window. He accelerates down the dirt path, heading towards him. The guy tilts his head out the window. "Close the door!" he shouts to his friend.

Before the lieutenant reaches the side of building, he sees Henry shutting the door. The man lifts his foot off the gas pedal and rolls fast down the roadway. He swerves left to the rear off the barn, sliding the tires.

Swiftly, Greg brakes to a stop by the back entrance. He puts the truck in neutral and climbs out in haste. He opens the rear barn doors all the way and props them with cinder blocks. The man hurries inside the barn and sees Henry peeking through a crack in the door.

Within seconds, his friend turns to him. "That damn convoy is lookin' like they're rushin' to a funeral." he says, "What's goin' on?"

"That's Moran's wife in the white car." Greg tells him, "I think her posse is following her."

"What are they up to?" Henry asks, curious.

"She's going to get her son." the lieutenant answers rushing to Ned's truck.

His friend strolls back to him as he lowers the trailer's landing gear, "You changin' trucks?" he inquires.

"Yeah." Greg replies disconnecting the cables from the trailer, "They know this rig. Hopefully, they don't remember the trailer number. I'm taking a chance with that."

"You're in this pretty deep, man." Henry says as the lieutenant hurries back to the cab.

"I gotta' get this load outta' here." Greg responds rushing inside the cab, "I don't wanna' put you in any danger."

The lieutenant starts the tractor and pulls away from the van. He drives it out of the barn and steers on the grass. The man engages the parking brakes and emerges from the vehicle. He runs back to Gary's truck and climbs inside.

Quickly, Greg backs inside and hooks to the trailer. He gets out of the vehicle and rushes to raise the landing gear. He connects the air hoses and light cable, and hears Henry coming behind him.

His friend approaches him and stands aside. "You be careful out there." he suggests and gives him a pat on the shoulder, "I wish I was back on the force to help ya' out."

"You're retired." the lieutenant responds, "Enjoy it."

Greg dashes back to Ned's truck. He climbs inside and parks it behind the building. The guy turns off the engine and leaves the key in the ignition.

Afterwards, he gets out and shuts the door. The lieutenant returns to his friend breathing rapidly. His attention is drawn to the small plastic bag in Henry's hand. "Thanks for everything." he says, "I couldn't have done it without you. I'll come back to get Ned's truck."

His friend shakes his hand. "You're one hell of a cop." he states, "I'd hire your ass any day."

"Thanks man." the lieutenant replies with a smile, "But I've got to finish the job."

"I know." Henry utters and hands the plastic sack to him, "Martha wanted you to have a little snack. It's a sandwich, soda, and potato chips. You know how she is."

"Tell her I'm sorry I didn't get a chance to say hello." Greg mentions to him with a grin, taking the bag, "I'll see you again soon. You know I will."

"I know." his friend says, "You watch your tail out there, and be careful."

Greg nods and slaps him lightly on the shoulder. "I'll be in touch." he adds.

Suddenly, their attention is drawn to a pickup parking next to Ned's truck.

Henry walks to the rear entrance and looks. "That's my truck." he recognizes it.

The lieutenant climbs inside Gary's semi-tractor. He lays the sack in the passenger seat and disengages the parking brakes. Swiftly, he shifts the vehicle in gear. As his friend moves out of the way, Greg rolls out of the building. He gives Henry a wave and pulls out far enough to get the trailer out. The guy steers right afterwards, and rolls out to get the van on the dirt path. He turns on the headlights and attaches his seatbelt quickly.

After a clockwise maneuver around the barn, the lieutenant checks the passenger mirror. He sees the tail lights of the trailer passing the corner of the building. The guy steers left toward the gate, and looks at the police car on the street. He realizes the vehicle trailed the officer driving Henry's truck.

Greg approaches the roadway and pulls out wide to steer around the parked vehicle. He turns left and gets the trailer aligned on the roadway.

Quickly, the lieutenant accelerates and drives away.

Chapter Twenty-Four

It's almost 2:00 a.m. in the morning, and Lieutenant Hardison is near the Langston Branch Road intersection. He's preparing to make a turn, heading back towards the food mart area. He finishes the last of his soda, and drops the can in the sack. Afterwards, Greg places the bag on the floor. The guy signals and begins reducing his speed.

Just feet before reaching the crossing, Ned's phone rings. The lieutenant pulls it out and looks at the screen. He sees Moran's name. The man's debating if he should answer the call. Finally, Greg stuffs it back inside his pocket.

The lieutenant stops at the intersection and notices a vehicle coming from his left. So the guy waits for it to pass. When the car goes by, the guy pulls out in haste. He steers right heading the same way. The lieutenant straightens the trailer on the roadway and *his* phone rings this time.

The man glances at the screen and answers the call.

"Hey, bro'." his brother greets him, "I'm calling to check on ya'. Also, I need directions. I'm gonna' let you explain them to Kim. I'll follow her lead."

"Let me pick a good spot first." Greg informs him, "I'll call you in about thirty minutes."

"Got it." Wade says, "We'll get setup and wait for Douglas's crew to get there."

"Give me some time." the lieutenant requests, "I'll contact Moran when we get every detail worked out."

"Will do." his brother agrees, "I thought you might like to know something else. I've been researching about Eleanor Moran again. I've made a few phone calls. The lady was discharged from rehab about a month ago. She was admitted into Kenson Rehab in Tampa nearly a year ago for spine therapy."

"Back problem?" the lieutenant figures.

"You can say that." the agent states, "A gunshot wound to the lower torso. She was admitted under her maiden name, Eleanor Leyton."

"She was probably trying to hide from Moran." Greg figures, "I believe that lady's been through hell because of him. If that bastard had found out his wife was still alive, he would've went after her to finish the job."

"Eleanor's staying at the Sunrise Hotel." his brother explains, "The bellman reported seeing a woman loading a couple of nickel-plated handguns in the hallway. The desk clerk called the precinct over an hour ago. He described her, and I faxed him a picture of the woman. The guy gave me a positive I. D. of the lady and the false name she's using, Diana Gateman. She has a driver license with that name on it. There's no record of anybody in Tampa with that name. The rehab facility identified her once *they* saw the picture I sent them."

"That's good work, bro,'." the lieutenant admits.

"There's more." Wade adds, "Adrian Leyton was reported missing two days ago. Guess who the babysitter was at the time of the disappearance?"

"Who?" Greg asks.

"Lori Caldwell." the agent answers, "the Florida senator's daughter."

"I'll be damned." the lieutenant responds, "Who was the child living with?"

"Alana Leyton." Wade relies, "Eleanor's older sister. She filed a missing report for both of them. The lady told the Tampa police that two masked men held her at gun point, and kidnapped Lori and the child."

"We know for sure he's got the female.' Greg says, "Captain Harris told us. Lori also admitted that the boy is there too. We have to find where Moran is keeping them."

"That sounds logical to me." his brother decides.

"Do me a favor?" Greg asks, "I'll give you a few minutes longer to do this."

"Okay." the agent concurs, "What's up?"

"Check to see if there are any properties here under the name, Adrian Leyton." the lieutenant requests, "They can't find Douglas under *his* name. Maybe it's listed like that. - Also, look up Tamela Perkins again. I hope you can find me some addresses."

"Sure, bro'." Wade says.

As his brother continues talking, something catches Greg's attention in the distance ahead. He's observing two black sedans passing under the street light, creeping through the intersection on Highway 51.

Mysteriously, the guy sees them turning into the food mart parking lot. "I gotta' go, man." he tells Wade, "There's something I have to take care of."

"You need some help?" the agent asks.

"Not right now." the lieutenant answers, "I can handle this one."

"We're here for you." his brother assures him, "I don't want you facing them alone."

"I'll be alright." Greg mentions, "I'll call back in about thirty to forty-five minutes."

They exchange goodbyes, and the lieutenant disconnects the call. He returns his phone to the case while staring the scene ahead.

Greg looks at the stop sign at the intersection. He glances to the left and right, seeing no other additional traffic flowing at this time.

Instantly, the lieutenant begins increasing his speed. He exceeds a couple of hash marks over seventy miles per hour and holds steady. He turns his headlights off, and takes a glimpse at the store.

In just a few seconds, Greg surges through the intersection. He checks his side mirror to see if they noticed him. The guy doesn't see anyone following yet. The lieutenant's approaching a left bend in the roadway. So he reduces his speed and turns his headlamps back on.

As the man steers through the curve, a thought dawns on him. "If all of those bastards know where the store is," he mumbles with a pause, "I don't have to tell Kim directions. She *knows* where it is. I can drop the damn trailer in the woods behind the building."

Suddenly, Greg spots a cement company on his right ahead. The fenced area is well lit with pole lights illuminating their row of mixer trucks. The guy gazes at the wide gravel trail, seeing it's large enough to turn around.

Swiftly, the lieutenant dips the truck into the entrance. He pulls up at an angle and straightens the trailer in the driveway. The man backs the van in completely.

Hastening, Greg drives out on the roadway again. He turns left, going back towards the food mart. "Hopefully, those cars are gone." the man utters, "I'll drive about twenty-five miles per hour. - That ought to give them enough time to get outta' there. The cashier said they're usually in and out quickly."

Shortly, the highway intersection is in view before him. It looks secluded, with no traffic flowing in either direction. The lieutenant starts slowing down, and coasts to the crossing. He veers his eyes to the store area and spots only one small car parked near the front doors. So the guy goes on through the intersection, staying on Langston Branch Road. He drives past the building and reaches the wood line. Greg notices a grassy farm path leading into the bushes. So he blindside backs the trailer in the trail, and goes all the way in the brush for concealment. He shuts his headlights off, still seeing no traffic in the area. The guy engages the parking brakes and emerges from the vehicle in haste. He rushes through the weeds and gets to the van.

Quickly, the man lowers the landing gear. The lieutenant disconnects the cables and returns to the cab. He disengages the truck brake knob and slowly drives away from the trailer.

Suddenly, his phone rings again. So the guy pulls out the brake knob again and answers the call with his earpiece.

"Hey, bro'," Wade says, "I got some info for ya'. There's one home registered to Tamela Perkins. But check this out. There's a huge house here under the name, Adrian Leyton."

"Hang on a minute." Greg asks and shifts the truck to neutral. He takes his foot off the brake pedal and stuffs his hand in a dashboard slot, looking for something to write with. He finds nothing. So the guy checks the overhead compartment and retrieves a handful of items. He takes a notepad and pen out then stuffs the other items back inside.

Greg feels for a flashlight in there, and finds a pocket-style type under Gary's glasses. He closes the overhead door quickly and holds the pad on the steering wheel. "What's the address to the home with his son's name?" he inquires.

"The house is at 4120 Forsythe Lane." Wade reads.

"I know where it is." the lieutenant remembers, "That's Dr. Forsythe's old home. His security alarm went off about four years ago. I answered the call and checked his property for him. He was Richard's primary physician, and one of his best friend's."

"That's very good man." his brother says, "Being familiar with the area is a plus."

After writing down the location, Greg tears the page out and stuffs it in his jacket pocket. He returns the pen and pad to the compartment then reattaches his seatbelt. "Here's the deal, bro,'." he begins to explain, "Don't tell the captain anything I'm telling you, okay?"

"You have my word." the agent agrees.

"Can you appoint somebody to receive the money from Moran?" the lieutenant asks turning off the overhead light, "They can't have the F. B. I. letters on their clothing at all. Let them wear plain clothes, and don't let him be wired. Douglas might check for that."

"I can take care of that." Wade assures him, "I'm having one of the guys to video the entire transaction. There'll be listening devices nearby, and a van in the woods to monitor them. You leave that to me."

"Okay." Greg responds, "He's got to be at that address. I'll lay money on it. The house is in a little town named, "Ardmore". It's about twenty miles south of here off Highway 51."

"I believe you're right." his brother replies.

"When Moran leaves the house?" the lieutenant says, "I'm going in."

"If you need backup sooner, don't hesitate to call." the agent voices bluntly, worrisome, "That's a dangerous move. And I wish you'd wait for us. I've got another team here to help us. They just got here."

"If those bastards see all of you, they're gonna' run." Greg explains, "And they'll take the hostages with them. I don't want that to happen. Keep the other team on standby for the old airfield. Nobody makes a move until the transaction is done."

"Alright." Wade tells him, "I'll see you after we get Moran. Love ya,' man. Just be careful."

"Love you too, bro'." the lieutenant says, "I've been busy with this mess since Friday night man. I couldn't even go home in peace. My goal is to keep my family safe. I don't give a damn if I have to stay out all night to make that happen. The threat has to stop man. If they want a war, I'll give "em one."

"I feel ya,' man." his brother agrees with him, "Do what you have to. Just stay safe. And I'll see ya' soon."

"Okay." Greg responds, "Is Kim there?"

"Yeah." his brother replies, "She's right here. Hold on a minute."

The lieutenant waits for her to come on the line.

"Hey, Greg," Detective Allison speaks, "what's up?"

"The trailer is at the corner of Highway 51 and Langston Branch Road." he informs her, "It's behind the food mart in the farm trail. You know where the store is, right?"

"Yeah." she replies, "I get gas there all the time. It's cheaper."

"Don't make a move until I give you a call." he instructs her, "When Douglas comes for the trailer, he's in your hands."

"We'll be ready." she assures him, "Be careful, my friend."

"I will." he says.

The two end their conversation and Greg disconnects the call. He grabs his bag and hurries opening the door again. The guy gets out of the truck and goes to the rear of the trailer. He opens one of the doors and stuffs the flashlight inside his pocket.

After slinging the bag, the lieutenant climbs inside the trailer. The guy maneuvers to one of the crates he'd opened earlier. He gets the flashlight out, and shines it on the box. Greg forces the wooden top aside and pulls out three grenades from the crate. He drops them inside his bag and gets down out of the van.

The man closes the trailer door and stuffs the flashlight inside his pocket. He hurries through the weeds and gets back to the cab. The guy takes the tote off his shoulder and climbs up to the driver seat. He sits and lays the bag on the passenger side.

Quickly, Greg slams the door. He disengages the parking brakes, and pulls the tractor on the roadway. The guy steers to the left and drives toward the intersection.

The lieutenant gets to Highway 51 and makes a right turn. He up shifts the gears rapidly and races down the highway.

Within minutes, Greg's approaches the old airfield. He looks to the left and notices flood lights on in the area.

There's illumination also in the windows of the warehouse, indicating that some activity is happening.

As the wood line thins more, the lieutenant sees a jet sitting on the runway.

It's nearly twice the size of a Lear model, resting with a black sedan beside it.

The man can see at least eight personal vehicles parked on the visible side, appearing as if a crew is conducting shift work.

Greg retrieves his phone from the case. He calls his brother back and waits for him to pick up.

"What's up man?" Wade greets him.

"There's definitely some activity going on at this old airfield." the lieutenant confirms, glancing aside, "It's on Highway 51, about a mile south of Quick Stop Food Mart. Kim knows where it is."

"When do you want us to hit the airfield?" the agent asks.

"Have them to stakeout in the woods behind the landing strip." Greg tells him, "If anybody tries to board the jet, tell the guys to move in. Otherwise, they wait until you do the transaction with Moran."

"Okay, bro'," Wade says and mysteriously hesitates, "Umm-"

The lieutenant becomes curious, "Is something wrong?" he asks.

"Your captain's following me man." the agent confesses.

"Richard's behind you?" Greg wonders.

"Huh, yeah." his brother admits, "He probably wants to talk to you. Let me stop. I don't want him to think I'm trying to get away."

Suddenly, he hears Richard asking if it's him on the line.

"Greg?" his boss says on the phone, "I already know what you're doing. You're disobeying my direct order, aren't you?"

"Umm-" the lieutenant sounds, wordless.

"You know?" Richard pauses and speaks bluntly, "Usually, the government takes over an investigation when they get involved. Wade's boss wants his teams to follow *your* lead. *Our* guys are backing them up. The F. B. I. director says the FAA tracked Rivera's jet taking off. They say it landed here, and he's probably going where you're headed. We're dealing with two ruthless son -of -a -bitches here. And I don't want you to get your ass blown off. If you weren't an army veteran like me, I wouldn't trust what you're doing. Stay safe and you *better* call for backup. That's an order."

"Yes sir." Greg acknowledges.

Wade returns on the phone. "I didn't say anything, bro'." he pleads, "It's not my fault."

"I believe ya'." the lieutenant states, "Richard knows me very well."

They exchange goodbyes, and Greg returns the phone to his pouch. He pulls out Ned's flip phone and sees the battery usage is at 62 percent. So the man stuffs it back inside his pocket. Greg checks his mirrors and notices no traffic on the highway. Gradually, the guy gets more comfortable and cruises on down the roadway.

Chapter Twenty-Five

Shortly, Lieutenant Hardison approaches his first turn at Crestwood Road. He brakes, and steers right onto the street. The man shuts off his headlights and drives on another hundred feet. He slows down before reaching the Forsythe Lane sign. Greg remembers a dirt trail used by a farmer years ago on the left. The path leads to an area where a corn field used to be. Nobody has farmed on it since the man passed away.

Carefully, the lieutenant looks for it under the moon's bright illumination. He spots two tire tracks leading into the woods.

Quickly, the guy stops and emerges from the vehicle. He hears multiple gunshots in the distance. He realizes the noise is coming from an area near the large home beyond the bordering trees. Greg returns to the tractor, and backs the vehicle in the grassy tire tracks. The guy continues moving in reverse until the truck is concealed by the trees and brush. He stops quickly and shifts the gear to neutral. The man pulls out the yellow brake knob and shuts off the engine.

Hastening, the lieutenant grabs his bag. He uses the available light inside the cab to go through some of his contents. The guy grabs a stocking cap with the eyes and mouth cut out. He pulls it over his head and adjusts it for a proper fit.

Afterwards, Greg reaches inside and lifts his automatic handgun out. The guy checks the weapon and pulls the top assembly back to cock it. He flips the lever off the safe mode and tucks the gun inside the rear of his belt.

The lieutenant opens the door. He drops the tote outside upon the grass. The man grabs the collapsed rocket launcher and does the same with it.

Swiftly, the man retrieves the rifle from the passenger side. He sticks the barrel out the opening and slides that way himself. The man lowers the weapon over his head stretching its strap across his chest. Hastening, Greg climbs down from the tractor. He closes the door and lifts the rifle off his body.

The lieutenant slings the straps of the bag and launcher across his front torso. He creeps away towards the gunfire with his SKS in hand. The man uses the trees for cover, following their elongated shadows before him. He moves on through stray weeds and bushes, being cautious with every step. After several feet, the guy notices the wood line thinning. He can see the lighted residence of the two story home, illuminated similar to a game field.

Suddenly, the sound of gunfire erupts again in the air before him. Greg can see a fierce battle starting to take place as he stares upon the vast lawn. The man halts behind a nearby tree, staring two teams of men shooting at each other. There's over a dozen vehicles on the house's lawn, with most of them cluttering the center. Instantly, the man shifts the rifle to his left hand. He retrieves his cell phone and calls the police dispatcher. He waits a couple of rings, and a female answers the line.

"I'm Lieutenant Hardison." he says, keeping his voice low, "Send two unmarked cars to the Forsythe Lane area. Have both to come westbound on Crestwood Road. Tell the officers to stop about fifty feet before the lane and pull off the roadway. I want their headlights off and their cars in the bushes. I'll call you with further instructions."

"Yes, sir." the lady responds, "I'll get right on it."

Greg disconnects the call and returns the phone to the case. He still has his eyes fixed on the tragic scene in front of him. Looking left, the man recognizes Eleanor's white Mercedes near the wood line. He also remembers the darker model coupes surrounding that car.

Suddenly, the lieutenant's attention is drawn to more black automobiles coming down the roadway to the home. As the gunfire ceases, he turns his eyes back to the prevailing crew left standing.

It appears they're assembling, focusing on the approaching convoy.

Mysteriously, the lieutenant hears gun shots in the house's back area. He follows with his eyes and spots Eleanor running to the rear of the home.

She turns around instantly and discharges rounds with her two handguns. Abruptly, the woman gets hit with a round in her left shoulder. She staggers and resumes shooting with her uninjured arm.

"Get her!" he hears and shifts his focus to Moran's voice at the front entrance. "Kill her and bring the body to me!" the villain orders with his magnum held down at his side.

Simultaneously, a few more guards join others chasing her as she dashes deeper in the woods.

Greg scales the tree line to reach her immediately. He's far enough inside the wooded area to keep concealed, hoping he can save her. The guy's working his way around the house without stepping on the lawn.

Shortly, the lieutenant reaches the rear wood line leading to the back yard. He races to catch the guards following Eleanor.

Just as Greg goes deeper in the tree bed, he hears a sudden burst of rounds behind him. He glances back over his shoulder and sees no one coming his way. So the lieutenant returns his focus to the bushes in front of him. He notices one of stalkers firing at the woman.

Swiftly, Greg halts and aims the rifle at the attacker. He fires two rapid shots and drops the man to the ground. He maneuvers his weapon quickly and shoots three more guys firing at her. The lieutenant watches their lifeless bodies descend to the patches of brush, still rushing to reach Eleanor.

Greg increases his speed, trying to catch up with her. He gets closer and she turns around in haste.

Immediately, the lady aims her gun at him.

"Eleanor!" he yells before the female fires, "Don't shoot! I'm here to help you!"

Instantly, the guy stops. He folds up his stocking cap, catching his breath.

Gently, the man holds the rifle up in his left hand. He opens his right palm, facing her.

"I'm here to rescue Lori Caldwell and your son." he says, "If Adrian is in there with her, I'll rescue him too."

"I saw you earlier at the police station." she remembers, "You're a cop, aren't you?"

"Yes." he answers, "But we're not going back there at all. I promise. All I need you to do is trust me."

"Why are you helping me?" the woman asks.

"I wanted to make sure your child has a mother." the lieutenant admits and checks the rear over his shoulder. He turns his eyes back to her. "You've been through enough, Eleanor. We want Douglas, not you. And I know he tried to kill you. I can clear you with all of this." he explains and points to the house, "If Adrian is in there, I'll get him."

Gradually, she lowers the handgun to her side.

Greg veers his eyes to her left shoulder. "You're losing a lot of blood." he mentions, "Let me get you to the emergency room. I'll make sure your son and car gets to the hospital with you. When you feel better? You two can go home, okay?"

Eleanor nods. "It's a war zone out there." she says, and pauses briefly catching her breath, "How can you get past all of them?"

"You leave that to me." the lieutenant assures her pulling out Ned's phone, "Disregard what you hear."

Greg pulls up Moran's name and calls him. The line rings twice and the mob boss picks up. "I've tried to call you!" Douglas yells with rage, "You've caused a lot of problems out here tonight! Where's my damn trailer, you son -of -a -bitch!"

"Do you have the money!" the lieutenant lashes back.

"Yes!" Moran exclaims, "Where's my merchandise!"

"Meet me at the wood line behind Quick Stop Food Mart!" Greg orders him, "That'll be on Langston Branch Road which crosses U. S. Highway 51! I'll be there waitin' for ya'! Do you know where that is?"

"I know where the damn place is!" the boss acknowledges in anger, "Just make sure the goods are there!"

"I'll be here waitin' for ya'!" Greg lashes back, "I like lookin' eye to eye with the one I'm doing business with! Show your manhood! Let me see you're not a coward!"

The lieutenant disconnects the call and returns the phone to his pocket. He looks at Eleanor leaning against a tree. Hurrying, the guy slings his rifle across his back. He approaches the lady and wraps her right arm around his neck. Greg grabs the woman's waist with his other hand and escorts her through the woods. He heads back towards the front, staying enough inside the tree line for concealment.

They reach the side of the house, and notice a convoy of black sedans storming up Forsythe Lane. There's a few guys left behind outside dragging corpses to a nearby white van.

While traveling along, Greg observes two of Moran's men dragging a live man towards the house. He veers his eyes to the yard and sees a second pair doing the same with another guy.

Suddenly, Eleanor tries to break away from him. He snatches her back as she aims the handgun at the front pair of men.

"That's my brother!" she blurts in a strong whisper.

"I'll get him!" the lieutenant responds keeping his voice low, "Just calm down!"

The lady stops resisting and hurries walking on with him.

Greg can see she's almost out of strength. The woman's leaning against him to stay on her feet. As they move through the brush, the lieutenant takes another glimpse at the scene. Again, the man stares at the two guys being escorted. "Who's the one being pulled behind your brother?" he asks.

"That's Rivera in the white suit." she says, "They must've ambushed him after he got here. Douglas's crew did the same to us. My brother pushed me away and told me to run. He spotted the second crew coming behind us. - Now I have to save him."

"I'll see what I can do with that." he tells her glancing at her drowsy eyes, "First, I have to get you outta' here. You're getting weak."

Immediately, Greg snatches out his phone. He dials police dispatch and waits for an answer.

Finally, a woman picks up the line and he remembers her voice.

"This is Lieutenant Hardison again." he responds, "I spoke to you earlier?"

"Are you ready for them?" she inquires.

"Just the first car." the guy explains, "Tell him to wait until the traffic clears. A group of black sedans are leaving right now. When they're out of sight, have him to pull past Forsythe Lane and stop on the shoulder. Send another unit to replace him. When they stake out tonight, I want them in pairs."

"Yes, sir." she replies, "Will do."

Quickly, Greg calls Wade. His brother picks up on the first ring. "What's going on?" he asks.

"Moran's on his way." the lieutenant informs him.

"Okay." the agent says, "We're ready."

"Keep me posted." Greg requests.

"You got it." Wade assures him.

"Do me a favor bro'." the lieutenant asks.

"Sure man." his brother agrees, "What's up?'

"Can you clear Eleanor's name from this mess?" he asks, "I want this lady to have a new life with her son. She's been through enough, - and you know it."

"I can get that done." the agent says, "You got my word on it."

"Thanks." Greg responds.

The lieutenant ends the call and tucks the phone back inside the case. He looks at Eleanor blinking her eyes slowly. "Stay with me now." he tries to motivate her, "Hang in there."

Shortly, the man passes Gary's truck. He continues on and spots a police squad car resting at end of the path.

The officer sees him coming and leans over to open the passenger door.

Greg arrives at the cruiser with the woman and carefully helps her get in. "Let me have your guns, Eleanor." He requests unzipping his bag. "You can't take those inside the hospital." the lieutenant tells her, "They'll be in your trunk when I return your car. - And remember, use your maiden name, Leyton."

The lady nods and gives him the weapon in her hand. She struggles to draw the other for him.

Cautiously, the lieutenant assists her without aggravating the injury. He places both handguns in his tote and zips it.

The policeman helps him secure her seatbelt, and he closes the door gently. "Get her to the emergency room A.S.A.P.," Greg tells him, "- and guard her. Call for a relief or backup if you need them. Eleanor goes home when she gets better. That's an order. Let everyone know. "

"Yes sir." the officer says.

"Turn around and go back the way you came here." the lieutenant says and steps back away from the vehicle, "Hurry!"

Before moving on, Greg gets his phone out and calls his wife. He steps back in woods to conceal himself as the squad car pulls away.

After a couple of rings, Janna answers. "I've been waiting for you to call, honey." she says, "I've been up worrying about you."

"I'm sorry, baby." he responds, "I'm still trying to resolve this matter."

"I know sweetheart." his wife replies, "The doctors said that Gary and Daddy are gonna' be alright, and Landon is asleep. We miss you."

Greg lowers his head. "I miss both of you too." he mentions sadly, "I wish this had never happened. – I'll be home as soon as I can."

"I know." she says, "Just be careful. - I love you, honey."

"I love you too." he responds.

They exchange goodbyes, and the man disconnects the call. He assures the phone is in the vibrate mode and stuffs it back in the case. Swiftly, the lieutenant lifts the rifle's strap over his head. He holds the weapon in his hands, briefly staring the grassy path.

After pulling the stocking cap over his face, the guy dashes down the trail. He moves on through the woods and heads back towards the home.

Chapter Twenty-Six

Within a few minutes, Lieutenant Hardison arrives in the wood line facing the side of the house. While staring at the front entrance, he works his way through the brush to get a better view. The man moves to the closest tree and conceals himself behind it. He sees one of the guards holding Eleanor's brother and the other beating him.

Just to the right of them, Greg notices a second pair of guards. They've badly beaten Rivera to unconsciousness.

Scanning his eyes farther to the right, he spots a crew conversing beside a black Lincoln sedan. Closest to him, the guy notices Eleanor's white Mercedes near the wood line. It's surrounded by vehicles driven by *her* guards who are now deceased, excluding Eleanor's brother. He realizes the majority of the security crew has left with Moran.

Quickly, Greg lays the rifle upon the grass. He pulls the rocket launcher over his head. The man detaches the front and rear covers, and drops them aside. He places a hand at each end, gazing at the group upon the lawn. The man extends the weapon swiftly, lifting the front and rear sights. Afterwards, the lieutenant lays it upon the grass.

The guy reaches aside and unzips his bag. He retrieves two grenades and places them near the brush.

Quickly, the lieutenant lifts the rifle. He shifts his aim to the guys beating Eleanor's brother. The guy shoots them, and immediately fires at the two standing over Rivera's body. He drops all four of them to the ground, lying motionless.

Greg turns to the men on the lawn, observing them drawing their weapons. Hastening, the lieutenant rests the rifle upon the grass. He raises the rocket launcher and points at the center most car. The guy squeezes the trigger and fires the flaring projectile.

The round disintegrates the sedan with a fiery blast. Afterwards, the man drops the empty weapon to the ground. The lieutenant grabs one of the grenades. He yanks the pin out and releases the clip with his thumb. The man stands quickly and throws it hard at the crowd. The bomb explodes brightly, flipping two of the last three vehicles.

Greg does the same with the second grenade, throwing at the group running away. A splattering eruption of fire appears with the blast, projecting their bodies in the air.

Suddenly, the sound of silence surrounds him. The man picks up his rifle in haste. He steps out of the woods and moves toward the home with a tactical aim. He glances at Eleanor's brother kneeling on the lawn. "Get behind the bushes and stay there." he tells him, "I'll come back for you. Your sister's alive, and wants me to save you."

"Okay." the guy agrees and hurries for cover.

Abruptly, two armed guards rush out the front door. The lieutenant fires at each one, dropping them to the porch. Immediately, a woman lunges out the entrance. She staggers down the steps, and falls on her side. The guy keeps his aim upon her, but doesn't shoot. He creeps on slowly, listening to her groan in pain.

Strangely, Greg recognizes the slender woman. He remembers the light-colored dress from an earlier incident at the police station. "Dr. Perkins." he mumbles to himself, and proceeds on.

Instantly, his attention is drawn to an arm reaching out the front door with a pistol. He shifts his barrel quickly and fires a round through the elbow.

The guard stumbles out the door and shifts the weapon to his other hand. He faces the lieutenant and raises the weapon.

Swiftly, Greg shoots another round into his chest, dropping him to the porch. In haste, the man does an eye scan around him for danger. He eases over to Dr. Perkins and reaches out his left hand to her.

Greg keeps his trigger hand intact, holding the butt off the weapon into his shoulder pit.

As the lady grabs his hand, he keeps a locked aim at the doorway. "I'm Lieutenant Hardison." the guy introduces himself as she stands to her feet, "Can I trust you?"

"Yes." she replies, "They won't let me go anywhere."

"Stay close behind me." he says.

The man releases her fingers and resumes his tactical approach. He goes up the steps with her trailing him closely. "Where are the hostages, Tamela?" the man asks.

"In the basement." she replies, "You've got to hurry. He'll be back soon."

Greg slings the rifle and draws his automatic handgun from his belt.

"Are there anymore guards in here?" he inquires bluntly, with his eyes fixed ahead with the aim.

"No." she answers following him, "Go straight ahead to the kitchen. The entrance is by the back door."

Greg shifts the gun into his other hand. He draws the revolver from his holster and gives it to her.

The lady takes the weapon and continues trailing him. "The man beats me." she explains with watery eyes, "Douglas won't let me leave. He found out I was at the police station. I didn't say anything about him."

Quickly, Tamela goes to a cabinet near the kitchen sink. She grabs a key off a hook and returns to him. "He keeps it locked." she says.

"Stay up here and guard the entrance for me." he requests, "Don't be afraid to pull that trigger if you have to."

The lady nods wiping tears from her eyes.

Greg takes the key and opens the basement door. He flips on the light switch, and proceeds down the stairs with his handgun down at his side.

The guy gets to the floor and stalls staring the children sitting on the sofa.

They're gazing back at him with tears in their eyes, appearing terrified. The girl's arms are wrapped around the young boy, sitting closely together with him.

Greg raises the cap, revealing his face. "I won't hurt you." he assures them stepping closer, "I'm Lieutenant Hardison with the Redwood Springs Police Department." the man identifies himself and looks at the girl, "Are you Lori Caldwell?"

"Yes." the teenager answers with a nervy voice.

The man turns his eyes to the boy. "Is he Adrian Leyton?" Greg inquires pointing an index finger at him.

She nods and wipes a tear from her cheek.

"I came to get you out of here." he says, "Both of you come with me, and stay close."

In haste, the girl escorts the child to meet him. Greg leads them to the stairs and hurries up to the entrance. He reaches the kitchen, and waits for them to join him.

Instantly, the lieutenant tucks the handgun back under his belt. He pulls the rifle back over his head and holds it in his left hand. The guy hurries detaching the magazine. He replaces it with a fully loaded cartridge from his bag. "We'll go out the back way." the man decides.

Greg opens the rear door and emerges with a combative aim. He sees it's clear and signals for the others to follow him.

In haste, the lieutenant heads for the woods. He gets to the home's corner and peeks around the wall. The man sees no threat in sight, so he waves for the others to come with him.

Immediately, the four of them dash to the trees. They race through the bushes and reduce to a fast walk when Greg does. The guy pulls out his cell phone and dials the police department. He stares the silent front lawn while waiting for an answer.

Shortly, the same lady picks up the line.

"This is Lieutenant Hardison again." he says to her, "I need the units to pull up past Forsythe Lane. Tell them to wait there."

"Yes sir." the female answers.

Coincidently, his phone rings while he's disconnecting the other call. He answers watching Rivera turning on his back.

"Moran got away." his brother informs him, "So the man's probably coming for the boy. The guy made the transaction, but we've still got the shipment. That's enough for us to bust him."

"What went wrong?" the lieutenant wonders.

"Douglas saw our guys moving in." Wade explains, "He raced up Langston Branch Road towards the Deer Creek intersection."

"Are the sedans with him?" Greg asks.

"No." the agent replies, "We've got them, and also the crew at the airfield. I've got some units chasing him right now. He turned on a dirt trail off Deer Creek Road. Kim found it on a map. She says the path leads to Highway 51."

"Back off and give him some space." the lieutenant says, "Let him come here."

"I hope you know what you're doing." his brother mentions, "That bastard just shot three of our agents, and one of your guys. Thank God they're still alive. We need to get *there* to help *you*."

"You will." Greg assures him, "Just grant me that request."

"You got it." Wade agrees.

The lieutenant returns the phone to his case. He looks back at Lori and Tamela. Greg tells the teenager to get in the first car with Adrian. He asks Dr. Perkins to get in the second vehicle.

Both of the females nod.

Quickly, the man reaches Gary's semi-tractor. He moves on up the path and spots both police cars at the end waiting. So Greg stops and lets them go by heading for the roadway.

As Tamela passes, she hands him the revolver he gave her.

The guy holsters the weapon and follows them to meet the officers. Shortly, the lieutenant arrives at the first car and slings his rifle. He opens the front and rear doors. Lori and Adrian hurry getting inside.

Greg shuts the doors and peeks inside the passenger window. "Go back down Crestwood Road." he instructs the officer, "Take the girl to the station, and deliver the boy to his mother at the hospital. Look for a patient named, Eleanor Leyton, and make sure they stay guarded. Call and tell the captain what you're doing."

"Yes sir." the policeman answers.

"Hurry!" the lieutenant orders him.

The officer screams his tires turning around. He races away after straightening the car on the pavement.

Greg rushes to the rear cruiser. "Take her to the police station." he orders the second officer, "Make sure Dr. Perkins stay guarded."

"Got it sir." the policeman responds.

"Now, follow your partner out of here." Greg tells him.

The lieutenant watches him storm away down the roadway. Immediately, the guy pulls his cap back down over his face. He scurries into the path and moves on returning to the home.

Shortly, Greg reaches the area of the woods beside the home. He scans the surroundings cautiously, and emerges out to the lawn. The lieutenant runs to the hedges where Eleanor's brother is hiding. "Are you still here?" he asks.

"Yeah." her brother answers standing.

"Come on." Greg tells him, and the guy follows him across the grass.

They get to Eleanor's car, and he hears someone moving behind him.

Instantly, the lieutenant turns around aiming his rifle. He notices Rivera low crawling toward them, about twenty-five feet away. He's groaning in pain, straining to pull himself.

Greg returns to his eyes to Eleanor's brother. "Check for keys in the ignition." he says and the guy does so.

The lieutenant waits until he nods. "Open the trunk." he tells him.

When the remote switch releases the lock, Greg reaches inside his bag. He pulls out Eleanor's guns and tosses them inside the compartment. The guy shuts the trunk quickly and points behind to the paved entrance. "Get in the car and drive away from here as fast as you can." the lieutenant tells him bluntly, "Turn left after you get to the roadway. Don't turn your headlights on until you pass the first curve. Make two right turns at the next intersections, and the highway will lead you straight to the hospital. Look for the patient, Eleanor Leyton, your sister. Now, get out of here."

The lieutenant watches the guy hurry inside the vehicle and start it. He continues observing as the guy throws grass behind him, spinning the tires.

Instantly, Eleanor's brother races out of the area.

Greg glances at Rivera's body again, now lying upon the stomach. Immediately, he dashes back for his surveillance area in the wood line. The guy gets in position, and kneels waiting patiently.

159

Chapter Twenty-Seven

Nearly ten minutes later, the lieutenant hears a car speeding towards the area. He watches the black sedan until it skids upon the lawn.

Abruptly, Moran gets out on the passenger side holding his nickel-plated magnum revolver. The man strolls toward the house with a look of rage upon his face.

Greg retrieves the final grenade from his bag and pulls the pin out. He releases the clip and throws it hard at the Lincoln Continental. As Douglas's dark-suited driver emerges from it, the bomb disintegrates the vehicle. The blast flings his body in a fiery blaze, dropping him to the ground.

Immediately, the lieutenant steps out of the woods aiming at Moran's head. "Hold it right there!" he yells, creeping towards him, "You're under arrest!"

The mob boss halts and faces him with the weapon down at his side.

"Drop the damn gun!" Greg orders him and stops.

"Or what!" Douglas exclaims sarcastically, "Are you gonna' shoot me!"

The lieutenant tightens his grip on the rifle. "If you raise that pistol at me, I'll drop you where you stand."

Moran hesitates, looking at him curiously. "Your damn voice sounds familiar." he says with an evil stare.

"Drop the weapon, Moran!" the lieutenant exclaims, keeping his locked aim, "I won't ask you again!"

Douglas continues looking eye to eye with him. "Show your face and we'll talk!" he demands angrily, "Take off the cap!"

Suddenly, Greg hears the sounds of sirens approaching a distance away. He keeps the butt of the rifle in his shoulder pit. The man uses his left hand and folds the cap up, revealing his face.

Instantly, Douglas raises the pistol at him and Greg fires two rapid rounds into the arm. The mob boss staggers away grabbing his shoulder..

Gradually, Moran recovers to his stance and shifts the weapon to his other hand. "You're the bastard who shot me in the woods three years ago!" Douglas shouts arrogantly, "I remember now! On Taylor-Bend Road! I've been waiting to run into you again!"

Immediately, Greg recalls the memory and rage storms his mind. "*You* murdered Rhonda and Karen!" he blurts out angrily, tightening his index finger on the trigger.

"And I should've killed you!" the mob boss yells back, "I don't know any damn Rhonda! She had Madison on her name tag!"

"That's her, you son of a bitch!" the lieutenant lashes at him, "I ought to pull this trigger and blow your damn head off right now!"

"Do it!" Moran dares him, "Are you scared you'll be charged with excessive use of force!"

Mysteriously, Greg notices Rivera crawling again in his peripheral vision.

The white-suited man is nearly twenty-feet away to his right, just beyond where Douglas is standing.

As the mob boss bashes him with vulgarities, the lieutenant notices Rivera reaching for something in the grass. The man doesn't want to take his eyes off Moran with the pistol. So he keeps his locked aim as the sounds of sirens move closer.

Douglas cocks his revolver down at his side. "You cops need to keep your noses where they belong!" he expresses with a groan, "That business was between Karen and me! You and that lady cop didn't have a damn thing to do with it! She deserved to die, and so do you!"

Just as Douglas raises the firearm, he hears a shot fire from a gun in Rivera's hand.

The flash startles the lieutenant, and he aims at the shooter immediately.

The white-suited man lowers the gun, and his upper torso drops to the lawn.

Quickly, Greg turns the weapon back to Moran. He observes Douglas's eyes staring the sky. The lieutenant sees a stream of blood flowing from a hole in the side of his forehead.

After staggering back a step, Moran's body plunges to the ground.

Gradually, Greg lowers his aim gazing at the villain lying upon the grass. He bows his head and breathes out a sigh of relief.

Suddenly, flashing blue lights illuminate through the trees and roadway. They're followed by several red glows emitting the same.

Within a few seconds, a swarm of police vehicles storm into the area.

The lieutenant takes another glimpse at Rivera, his body still motionless and stretched out on the lawn. Shortly, he sees the captain's car halt on the grass before him.

Richard emerges from the vehicle in haste, drawing his weapon.

Wade skids to a stop next to him, and Detective Allison rushes out of the car first with a firearm in her hand. Agent Harrison steps out of the vehicle afterwards and turns back to his crew. "Clear the area!" he orders them, "Check the woods and every area of the home! I want all of their asses out here!"

Shortly, Captain Harris approaches Greg. "Are you alright, man?" he asks giving him a light pat on the shoulder.

Yes sir." the lieutenant answers slinging the rifle on his shoulder, "You can close the cold cases with Rhonda and Karen. Moran killed them. – He was the man I shot in the woods. He just confessed before Rivera shot him."

"His lawyers can't save him anymore." Richard utters glancing down at Douglas's body, "Vicious bastard."

"We've got a live one over here, sir!" an officer exclaims, drawing their attention, "He's beat up pretty bad! If the man doesn't get help, he's not hanging out long!"

Greg looks at the officer kneeling beside Rivera's body. He observes quietly as the paramedics rush to give the man medical attention.

Richard places his hand upon the lieutenant's shoulder. "Do you need to be checked out by EMS?" he asks.

"No." Greg replies, noticing Wade and Kim coming to meet them, "I'm just exhausted and hungry."

"You've done enough out here." the captain says, "They'll clean up this mess. Go get some rest with your family. I'll see ya' Monday morning."

"Thank you, sir." the lieutenant agrees, "I have to get Gary's truck back to the house. My car's over there."

"Where is it?" Richard inquires, lowering his hand to his side.

Greg points. "It's up there near the intersection." he responds, "It's in the grassy trail."

"I'll give you a ride." Captain Harris offers, holstering his gun.

"Kim approaches and gives him a hug. "Are you alright?" she inquires releasing him.

"I'll be fine." he tells her and points to Moran's body, "He confessed to killing Rhonda and Karen. I *did* shoot the bastard on Taylor-Bend Road. He told me."

Detective Allison stares at Douglas lying upon the lawn. "Finally." she pauses, "We get closure for the deaths." Kim turns back to Greg and gently places her hand upon his chest. "It's over." she says softly.

Wade pats him on the arm. "We'll take care of the rest, bro'?" the agent assures him, "You go home to your family. I know you're tired."

"I'll be okay." the lieutenant tells him, and gives him a thumb-wrap handshake. "I need you and chief to do me a favor."

"Sure." the agent says, "What is it, man?"

"Let Eleanor and her brother go." Greg requests, "They were defending themselves, and she needs to go home with her son. The lady's been through enough."

"You got it, bro'." his brother agrees, "You've helped us a lot. Thanks. I'll see ya' before I leave."

The captain taps him. "Let's get out of here." he suggests.

Greg hugs Kim again, and pats his brother's shoulder with short smile. They exchange goodbyes, and he gives them a final wave while turning away.

The lieutenant steps away with Richard, heading to his vehicle. Greg gets to the rear door and opens it looking at the crowd working in the area. He places his rifle and bag on the back seat, and stands in a short daze.

"Are you alright?" Richards asks, observing him from the driver's side.

The lieutenant nods and they get inside the car.

Captain Harris steers around the police cruisers and emergency vehicles. He pulls onto Forsythe Lane, and moves on towards the intersection.

Shortly, Richard arrives at the crossing and stops. He turns with a sigh, and shakes Greg's hand. "We couldn't have done it without you, man." he mentions, releasing his grip. "I want to thank you too."

"You're welcome, sir." the lieutenant replies, "It had to be done."

"You'll be the acting captain Monday morning." Richard informs him, "And Kim will be your lieutenant. I'm putting her in for a promotion. – I'm sure the mayor will approve it."

Greg smiles, "Okay sir."

The lieutenant gets out of the car and retrieves his belongings from the rear seat. He shuts both doors. After the man slings his items upon his shoulder, he pulls out the trucker's phone. The guy peeks inside the passenger window and hands it to the captain.

"Can you give this to Ned for me." he asks, "His truck is at Henry's house. The key is in the ignition. Can you handle that for me, Richard?"

Captain Harris giggles and grabs the mobile device from him. "I got it, man." he says.

Greg steps away and heads down the grassy path. He takes a final glimpse back, watching his boss drive away. Gradually, the lieutenant returns his eyes to the ground before him and takes a deep breath. He exhales slowly and wipes his forehead with a palm. "Damn." he mumbles to himself, "I'm glad this is over."

Greg reaches the tractor and his phone rings. He answers it stepping to the passenger door.

"I'm Officer Davis, sir." the man says, "You asked me to call when I get the boy to the hospital. I forgot. – I'm sorry."

"I remember." Greg recalls.

"He's with his mother,-" the policeman informs him, "and everybody's fine. We've got our eyes on them."

"I appreciate it." the lieutenant tells him, "Thanks. If you get tired, call dispatch for a relief."

"No problem, sir." the officer responds.

Greg presses his earpiece and disconnects the call. He puts his items inside the cab and heads around to the driver side.

The man climbs in the truck and starts the engine. As the vehicle goes through its cycles, the lieutenant retrieves the automatic handgun from his belt. He places it inside the bag and connects his seatbelt. The guy closes the door gently with a long sigh.

Suddenly, he goes into a brief daze, thinking while the tractor idles.

"It's time to go." Greg whispers to himself, snapping out of it.

So he pushes in the brake knob and shifts the truck in gear. He turns on his headlights and rolls toward the roadway. The lieutenant gets to the end of the trail and waits for another approaching ambulance. The man watches the flashing lights silently as the vehicle reduces its speed.

Rapidly, the emergency vehicle swerves down Forsythe Lane.

Greg pulls out his cell phone and calls his wife. He returns the device back to the case and pulls on the highway. He listens to the rings through his earpiece while making a right turn. As he upshifts moving on the roadway, Janna answers nervously.

"You don't have to worry anymore, honey." the lieutenant assures her, "I'm on my home."

"Finally, we can get some rest." she says, suddenly feeling relieved, "Thank God. It's been a long night."

"Yes it has." he agrees, "It's been a long night here too, baby."